GOD'S CHURCH AT ITS BEST

Stafford North

God's Church at Its Best
ISBN: 978-0-89098-438-3

©2019 by 21st Century Christian
Nashville, TN 37215
All rights reserved.

All rights reserved. No part of this publication may be reproduced, stored in a retrieval system, or transmitted in any form or by any means—electronic, mechanical, photocopy, recording, digital, or otherwise—without the written permission of the publisher.

Scripture quotations marked (ESV) are from the Holy Bible, English Standard Version® (ESV®), copyright © 2001 by Crossway, a publishing ministry of Good News Publishers. Used by permission.

Scripture quotations marked (NIV) are taken from the Holy Bible, New International Version,® NIV.® Copyright © 1973, 1978, 1984, 2011 by Biblica, Inc.™ Used by permission of Zondervan. All rights reserved worldwide. www.zondervan.com The "NIV" and "New International Version" are trademarks registered in the United States Patent and Trademark Office by Biblica, Inc.™

Cover design by Jonathan Edelhuber

▸ PREFACE ◂

I was baptized in 1941, almost 80 years ago. Since that time, I have observed and preached for churches all over the United States and in many foreign countries. Since 1963, I have been a member of the Memorial Road Church of Christ, formerly the College Church of Christ, located next to Oklahoma Christian University. During those years I have served as the education minister, the college minister, a deacon, a Bible class teacher, and an elder. Though I didn't realize it at the time, all these experiences were preparation to write this book with suggestions that can help churches be better.

All four of my children along with my wife, Jo Anne, have helped me with various chapters of this book, and Mark Taylor, Executive Minister at Memorial Road, has made helpful suggestions. My thanks to all of them.

God wants each congregation of His church to be the best they can be, and it is my hope that this book will help many of them to become that.

~ Stafford North

▶ TABLE OF CONTENTS ◀

Preface 3

Introduction 7

CHAPTER 1
How the Church's Mission Can Be Its Best 13

CHAPTER 2
How the Elders Can Be Their Best 19

CHAPTER 3
How the Deacons and Ministry Directors Can Be Their Best 37

CHAPTER 4
How the Preacher's Work Can Be Its Best 43

CHAPTER 5
How the Bible School Program Can Be Its Best 51

CHAPTER 6
How the Missions Program Can Be Its Best 65

CHAPTER 7
How the Local Outreach Program Can Be Its Best 73

CHAPTER 8
How the Benevolence Program Can Be Its Best 85

CHAPTER 9
How the Youth Ministry Can Be Its Best 95

CHAPTER 10
How the Women's Ministry Can Be Its Best 101

CHAPTER 11
How the Men's Ministry Can Be Its Best 111

CHAPTER 12
How the Ministry for Young Adults Can Be Its Best 117

CHAPTER 13
How the Ministry for Older Members Can Be Its Best 125

CHAPTER 14
How the Buildings and Grounds Ministry Can Be Its Best 133

CHAPTER 15
How the Worship Ministry Can Be Its Best 139

CHAPTER 16
How a Church's Website Can Be Its Best 153

CHAPTER 17
How the Fellowship at Church Can Be Its Best 161

ACTION 167

▶ INTRODUCTION ◀

In Ephesians 3:8-10 Paul says that he preached the eternal purpose of God, which was "made known through the church." Thus, before the beginning described in Genesis 1:1, God had in His mind a plan to save those who sinned. That plan meant sending His Son to die, and that plan involved a body of the saved to which each newly saved person would be added. Thus, the church which Christ built upon the truth that He was the Christ is the final step in God's eternal plan. We who are members of the church of Christ are participants in this eternal plan of God, and we should do our best to make our local unit of that church to fulfill God's purpose for His saved people.

God wants many qualities built into the local church to make it what He wants it to be. In this book we shall mention many of them and tell specific ways in which a local church can make itself the best that it can be.

A quick look at two congregations in the early church will give us a glimpse of excellent churches at work. First, we'll examine the church in Jerusalem. The first congregation of the church Christ established was in the city of Jerusalem, and the early chapters of Acts describe it clearly. Here is a list of things we are told they did well.

1. **This church preached the gospel.** Peter started this church with his message on Pentecost when he told those who believed his message about Christ that they should "repent and be baptized . . . for the forgiveness of your sins" (Acts 2:38, NIV). In the next chapter, we find another sermon Peter preached seeking to bring people to Christ, and in Acts 7, we find another a great sermon—this one from Stephen. Although it led to his death at the hands of angry Jews, Stephen was

willing to die for the cause. Churches today should seek effective preaching from their pulpit. Acts 2:42 says "they devoted themselves to the apostles' teaching." God help us to do the same! To be an effective church, we must stay with the teaching of the apostles, not adding to or taking from those teachings. We must refrain from using any doctrines or practices that came along later and should simply use the New Testament church as our model in everything. We should ask the question, "What did the early church teach and practice?" Since the apostles, led by the Holy Spirit, directed the church in the first century, we can be sure their approved teaching and practice was what God wanted it to be. Thus, when people ask why we teach this doctrine or why we don't do something other religious groups do, the answer should simply be —"Because that's what the early church taught" or "That's the way the early church did it."

2. **That leads us to the second characteristic churches should have: This church should be totally devoted to Christ, even willing to suffer and die for His cause.** Stephen and James were killed. Peter and John were imprisoned as were many others through the early years of this church. Acts 8:3 tells that "Saul began to destroy the church, going from house to house, he dragged off men and women and put them in prison." But why were they so willing to suffer? It was because of their total devotion to the cause of Christ, and we should be building into our members a similar commitment. If one would be willing to die for his faith, surely he should be willing to share his faith.

3. **The church in Jerusalem practiced effective worship.** Acts 2:42 says they devoted themselves to the breaking of bread and prayer. And in Acts 4, we read about a group of them gathering to give thanks for the release of Peter and John. In Acts 12, when Peter was again in prison, Christians gathered in the house of Mary, Mark's mother, praying for his release—and when an angel freed him, Peter came to that very house. Our worship services, therefore, should not only follow the New Testament plan for worship, but should also reflect our commitment to make our worship the best it can be in praising God and encouraging one another. As a byproduct of such worship, the worshiper will also be blessed.

4. **The Jerusalem church also had an extremely active benevolent program.** Many poor were among them, and some who had come to Jerusalem for the Passover feast, after being converted, stayed much longer than they anticipated. Members who had houses and lands sold them and gave the money to the apostles so they could give it to those with needs. And when, according to Acts 6 some of the Grecian widows were not being treated fairly, the apostles asked the members to choose men whom they could appoint to assure that all the widows were receiving proper care. Generous members helped those among them in need.

5. **And evangelism.** They started on the day of Pentecost with about 120 and then on one day, 3,000 were baptized. When Peter healed a crippled beggar, people came together, and he preached to them: "Many who heard the word believed, and the number of men grew to about five thousand" (Acts 4:4). When Peter and John were called before the Sanhedrin, which told them not to tell about Jesus anymore, they replied, "We cannot help speaking about what we have seen and heard" (Acts 4:20). And the number kept on growing as members kept on telling. After the persecution became more severe under Saul, many left Jerusalem for their safety, but everywhere they went, they kept sharing the message. Imagine Christians who had to leave home because of persecution continuing to tell about Jesus as they went to new places rather than keeping quiet for fear that they might be persecuted again. What a great example of commitment to evangelize!

6. **Another important practice of this church in Jerusalem was fellowship.** Acts 2:42 says they continued "in fellowship." Some think that was the giving element of their worship, and perhaps it was. The term, however, certainly indicates the close ties they had with one another and so does the way in which they took care of one another. When those close ties were threatened by the disagreement over the distribution of food to the Grecian widows, the apostles stepped in quickly to keep the rift from growing and found a way to bring peace again. A quick glance at 1 Corinthians shows Paul teaching a divided church about love because he knew that if they would truly love one another, they would quit their disunity over who had the greatest spiritual gift. So, churches today should take wise actions to build fellowship within the church.

7. **Although they didn't have a formal public relations program, what they did kept them in favor with all the people** (See Acts 2:47). And "everybody living in Jerusalem" knew about the miracles the apostles were doing. By whatever means available, then, the church made known what it was doing well in its city.

So the church in Jerusalem had programs for preaching, developing devotion to Christ, worship, benevolence, evangelism, fellowship, and public relations. And we only have an abbreviated record of what they did.

And now comes the church in Antioch. This church was planted by those from Jerusalem who were scattered by the persecution (Acts 11:19). Here the message was brought not only to Jews, but to Gentiles as well. And a great number believed. The apostles sent Barnabas to check things out, and he approved of what he found and encouraged them to remain true to the Lord (Acts 11:22-24).

1. The church had **a preaching ministry**, for Barnabas brought Saul from Tarsus to help with the teaching.

2. The church had **a benevolence ministry** because they sent a gift to Jerusalem Christians to help during a famine (Acts 11:29).

3. While the church was engaging in worship and fasting, the Holy Spirit sent them a message that Barnabas and Saul should go on a mission trip. So they were **a worshiping church**.

4. And their **mission program** became the headquarters from which Paul did his three missionary journeys.

Again we don't know all the church in Antioch was doing, but we know that they had active ministries for many important works. While serving under the apostles who had God's guidance through the Holy Spirit, then, these churches had carefully planned work overseen by good men. We also learn from these and other New Testament churches, that each congregation was told to hold firmly to the truth of the gospel while spreading the word, caring for its members, worshiping the Lord, and serving others.

Now here we are today. We must stay with the message the apostles preached and must model our teaching about how to become a Christian after what they taught. We must worship as they did and model our organization after theirs. We can use these early churches as examples for how we should be serving. We have to meet new circumstances, of course, but these early churches are our guiding light.

In this book, we shall embark upon a journey to find what the church should be doing and important keys to doing that work well. I have collected ideas from others and used my 70 years in preaching and 47 years as an elder to offer suggestions about the basic ministries every church should have. **Look at the ideas in each chapter to find the best ones for you to try.** Just as a race car does not get from zero to a 100 in an instant, your church will not be able to get from where it is to *the best it can be* in a week or even in a year. You can, however, select from the list of possibilities in each chapter those things that can best move you forward to the next level. When you have made those improvements, then take a look at this book again to get ideas about additional improvements to make.

Each chapter starts with a brief biblical basis for a particular ministry and then provides specific, practical ideas that churches, large and small, can do to be more like God would like them to be. Elders may want to choose next steps to take, or deacons with responsibilities in certain areas may look for ideas in their particular realm of work. Ministers may even look for ways to improve their own work or to suggest ideas to elders and directors of ministries. Ultimately, anyone working in a ministry should look for ideas about how that particular ministry might be made stronger.

Please note the last few pages in the book called "Action" before you start reading from the first. These pages will give you a systematic way of noting those items you believe would be good to implement. You should put a checkmark by the item as you read it, then go to the back, note the page, write a brief description of the item you want to start, and then write in the name of the person who would need to initiate the process of implementing that action. If that person is you, then write down "me," and if it is the elders or a particular person, then write those names. When you finish reading the book, you will then have a "to do" list about implementing those ideas you considered valuable while reading the book.

Some other ways to utilize good ideas from the book would be for church leaders to have a weekend retreat during which time they consider six or eight important ministries. In advance, they can provide copies of the book to those coming and then have discussion groups for those in various ministries to see what ideas the participants think are the best steps to take. The next step is key! They should decide on the best way to move from getting ideas in mind to putting such ideas into practice. The new practice won't get done unless a specific plan is made and given to someone to carry out. Then the person to whom the idea is assigned must have to report within the next month on what is happening about getting it started.

So each congregation should seek to be God's Church at Its Best. As seen in the New Testament, God wants each congregation to be His agent for spreading the Word, for worshiping Him, and for serving others. Now move through the rest of the book to get ideas so your congregation can be its best.

~ Stafford North

CHAPTER 1

THE CHURCH'S MISSION
Can be its Best

Jesus was strong on having a clear "mission." After His resurrection, He told His apostles to "Go, therefore, and make disciples of all nations, baptizing them in the name of the Father and of the Son and of the Holy Spirit, teaching them to observe all that I have commanded you" (Matthew 28:19-20, ESV). Mark records Jesus' mission statement this way: "Go into all the world and proclaim the gospel to the whole creation. Whoever believes and is baptized will be saved but whoever does not believe will be condemned" (Mark 16:15-16). In Acts 1, just before He ascended, Jesus said, "you will receive power when the Holy Spirit has come upon you, and you will be my witnesses in Jerusalem and in all Judea and Samaria, and to the end of the earth" (v. 8).

So our mission is to "go" to all the world—locally and in places far away—where we are to "make disciples"(learners, followers), and having brought them to the point of faith, we are to "baptize" them. Then our work continues as we "teach" these baptized believers all that Jesus has taught. Peter describes it like this: After one becomes a Christian, that person is to "Grow in the grace and knowledge of our Lord and Savior Jesus Christ" (2 Peter 3:18).

These statements tell us that the mission of each congregation of the Lord's church is

(1) to spread the message about salvation through Jesus in the most effective ways possible;

(2) when people are brought to faith, we are to baptize them into Christ; and

(3) following that we are to help them to grow by learning all that He taught. In so doing Christians will grow in the grace and knowledge of Christ. So, make disciples, baptize, and teach!

Expanding on this, we might say that a congregation should have an outreach both locally and in far-away places to spread the message of Jesus in the most effective ways possible. Having made believers, they should baptize them into the family, and then the congregation should find effective ways to help these Christians to grow toward maturity in knowing the Word and in serving Christ as they join in achieving the mission of the church. From Hebrews 10:25 and Acts 20:7 we also learn that Christians are to assemble regularly, and 1 Corinthians 14 teaches that in those assemblies we pray, teach, and sing praises so we can offer thanksgiving and strengthen one another.

Other passages that help us define another aspect of our mission are Acts 6:1-6 (feeding the Grecian widows), Galatians 6:10 (do good to all, especially to the household of faith), and 1 Timothy 5:3-16 (tells the church how to care for widows). From these passages, we know that an important function of New Testament churches was benevolence.

Putting all of this together, then, the mission of each congregation is

(1) to have a strong program of outreach to spread the gospel both near and far and, as a climax to this teaching, the congregation should baptize into Christ those who have believed;

(2) the congregation should have a strong, well-developed program to educate, encourage, and engage all members in serving;

(3) the church should have a program of benevolence to help its own members and others, and

(4) the church should conduct regular worship on the Lord's Day to honor, thank, and praise God. Every congregation should focus on these four goals and so should direct all of its efforts to achieve them. Every program, every dollar, and every effort should be aimed at achieving these four goals.

In achieving its mission, there are some strategies each congregation will find helpful. It is easy to stray into other directions and fail to keep these four scriptural items at the heart of all we do.

1. **Develop a mission statement.** In recent years, churches, businesses, schools, and even individuals have started to write a short, strong sentence that encapsulates their mission. They post such statements on their website and around their building. Each congregation of the church would benefit from developing such a statement. Basically the statement should tell what the church is going to do in following Christ's challenge to "go, disciple, teach, and praise."

   Here are a few samples taken from and adapted from some online church mission statements:

   - Knowing Jesus and making Jesus known.
   - Reaching up, reaching out, and reaching in.
   - Connecting people to Jesus and to one another.
   - To help people become fully devoted followers of Christ.
   - To bring people to Christ, to help them grow and serve.
   - To bring people to Jesus, develop them into Christ-like maturity, and equip them for their ministry.
   - To make disciples, baptize them, and prepare them for their ministry.

   So a church should develop a short statement that all the members can memorize that clearly defines what they hope to achieve. Once you have it, post it, mention it often in services and in your bulletin, and build your educational program and your preaching around it. Use it to promote your contributions. Develop it well, and publish it widely.

2. **Each year during the planning period for the coming year, all the ministries in the church should write specific goals for the coming year that connect with the four basic aims of the church.** If the ministry had objectives for the previous year, they should assess how well they did them and then should state what objectives their ministry plans for the year to come. These objectives should be in statements that are measurable so the target can be clear and their assessment specific.

If they require additional funding or manpower beyond what that ministry already has, this information should be presented in the report.

So, rather than stating an objective as "to grow attendance for the Sunday morning Bible school," the objective would be stated like this: "to increase Sunday morning Bible school attendance by 10 percent." As another example, an objective might be "to improve communication with our overseas missionaries by emailing or communicating with them via Skype once each month of the year." The ministry would then follow each of its objectives with a list of the ways it will work to achieve that objective. Here is an example. If the objective was to increase Sunday morning Bible school attendance by 10 percent, the committee might list such things as the following as its plan to reach that objective:

(1) Check the class attendance each Sunday and note members not present. If they miss two weeks in a row, a designated person will check with them to see if they are doing OK and to encourage them to be back soon.

(2) Class members will be asked to share the names of any who are not currently attending who might be contacted in a positive way about attending the class.

(3) Local visitors to the class will be asked to complete a card giving their name, email address, phone number, and physical address. A person designated to make visitor contacts will make the appropriate follow-up visit or call to encourage the visitor to return.

(4) Members of the class will be asked to think of people who have fallen away or who are not members of the church who might be prospective class attenders. Class members will be given an invitation card to the class and will be asked to make contact with such prospects to invite them to the class.

(5) Local people who visit church services will have an appropriate follow-up call to try to get them to come to church and to a Bible class.

(6) Topics will be chosen for Bible classes to study for a term that would be of special interest to those in the community not currently attending the church. Such topics can be advertised on the church's website, social media pages, or in the local paper; by e-blasts or mailings to the community; and by members sharing the information about the topic with their contacts.

Every quarter each ministry should assess how well it is moving toward its targets. Thus, they can check to see if they are making progress toward their goal, assess the effectiveness of efforts they are making, and think of additional ways they might go about achieving their objectives.

As they are planning for the following year, the ministry will determine how well it is achieving the objectives they set for the current year, report that to the elders, and then will make appropriate objectives for the following year. This process of setting objectives, checking regularly on progress, adjusting as needed, evaluating the objectives at the end of the year, and setting new objectives for the coming year is a beneficial way to proceed with the work of the church. To get each ministry to do this will require some training and a clear expectation from the elders to follow this plan. Someone trained in writing such objectives may need to meet with each ministry to help them as this process is getting started.

3. **Each three to five years, a congregation should do some long-range planning.** A committee composed of some elders, deacons, and ministers, along with a few others, should direct this effort. They might begin by proposing to the eldership an overarching statement of goals for the church over the coming period of time. Then each ministry should be asked to write a statement of what they can contribute to achieving these overall goals along with what manpower would be needed to carry out their proposal and how much their plan would cost.

Based on the information submitted, the overseeing committee would pull these reports together into a recommendation to the elders. They probably would do well to discuss some things with the elders as they move along because they should not go to the elders at the end with a big surprise. They will want to prioritize proposals and note the sequence in which they might be carried out. They might, for example, propose the addition of another paid minister to help carry out elements of the program in the second year, noting the cost involved at that point. They would also note any changes proposed for facilities and would set some intermediate targets to show progress along the way.

They then would present their proposal to the elders who would review the plan, note changes in staff, facilities, and any other additional expenses. They might accept the proposal as given or make modifications. The bottom line from this process would be a plan for some years to come, and each ministry would be asked to make its objectives to fit the larger picture.

Of course, the last step in this process is selling the plan to the church. This might begin with a meeting of deacons and ministry directors to seek their input and support. They might be given some time to digest it and discuss it with others in their ministry. Then the plan could be introduced to the church either at a special meeting or at a meeting of all adult classes on Sunday morning or on a Wednesday night or as part of the regular Sunday morning service. The plan should challenge the congregation to do more and give more and should be presented to show the great progress they would be making toward the basic things the congregation should be doing—outreach with the gospel, educating and helping the members to serve, benevolence, and bringing praise to God. The steps to achieving the plan should ask the members to take good steps forward, but should not ask what is beyond what they are likely to accept.

So, just as Christ and New Testament writers tell what the mission of the church should be, each congregation should be developing its own plan for how it will be achieving the scriptural mission of the church—to disciple those who are not Christians, to develop its members spiritually, to help the needy, and to be a temple of praise to God.

Many of the items mentioned in the following chapters could become part of a plan which a congregation might choose to develop. So, set a goal, and then keep your eyes on the goal.

CHAPTER 2

HOW THE ELDERS Can be Their Best

Christ's design for each congregation of His people is for them to have elders, qualified men who are set apart for leadership in His church. First Timothy 3 and Titus 1 are specific in listing the qualifications for these men, and a congregation should only choose men with these qualities. Since the New Testament always speaks of the elders in a congregation in the plural, a church should always have two or more elders. The Lord didn't want one individual to be able to impose his will on members of His church.

The New Testament uses three different words for those who lead the local congregation. They all appear in 1 Peter 5:1-2—"To the **elders** among you, I appeal as a fellow elder, a witness of Christ's sufferings and one who also will share in the glory to be revealed. Be **shepherds** of God's flock that is under your care, serving as **overseers**."

Peter refers to men serving in this leadership role as elders, because they are older and more experienced. This means they are prepared to give advice and make decisions about the work of the church. They can use their experience as a group in dealing with issues and in making plans, and they can use what they have learned over time to counsel individuals. Helping individual members with needs and problems should always be part of what elders do. They should get well acquainted with the members and be available to them for counseling. In a large congregation, the elders may be assigned to work with particular groups such as a class or a small group to make themselves better acquainted and more easily available.

Next Peter uses the word *shepherds*. Think of how shepherds treat sheep. The Holy Spirit did not guide Peter to call elders "cowboys" who rope a steer, throw him to the ground, and burn him with a branding iron. *Shepherds* indicates the tenderness and kindness these leaders will use in working with the members who are their flock. They go after the lost one, place him on their shoulders, and bring him back to the fold. They protect the sheep from wolves and bears—a figure for false teachers. They lead the sheep to find good pasture and plenty of water. So these leaders feed their flock well on the Word of God.

And finally, Peter uses the word *overseer*. Sometimes this word is translated as "bishop." An overseer is a manager. The word was used to describe managing a business or a vineyard, and it speaks of one who leads others to do their work well. Thus, the overseers of the church know what needs to be done and manage those for whom they have oversight to achieve those ends.

So we might summarize the work of elders with these three words—an *elder* or advisor, a *shepherd* or one who cares for the flock, an *overseer* or one who manages. The leaders in the church should be doing all three of these functions, and each man in this role should ask if he is balancing these three functions properly. Some go to meetings and help make decisions, but do not have much contact with the individuals they should be helping. Each eldership should occasionally ask, "Is each of us serving fully in the role God has given us?" If not, they should work on a plan that will help them to do that.

These elders, shepherds, overseers help the members know the Word, keep the faith, serve others, and spread the gospel. They also always need to work in harmony with one another. One of the most important things elders can do in a congregation is to promote peace among the members. Harmony among the leaders is a big step toward doing this. Often congregations will model the spirit among the elders. If they sense that the elders get along with one another working together harmoniously, then they will tend to develop that spirit. If they sense that the elders quarrel a lot, then they will tend to pick up that spirit as well, and the congregation will become divided.

The Bible does not tell us what to do if there are not qualified men to be elders over the congregation. This is probably so that a congregation will not take a substitute plan and use it permanently. But until there are qualified men, a congregation may have a meeting of the men or of all the members and select a steering committee of people who will handle some of the things elders would have done. Under their planning, this group can see that qualified people are responsible for the different ministries in the church. Though this committee does some of what elders would have done, they should not take on the role of substitute elders. They should have regular meetings with the members to ask their advice and to report on what they are doing. Certainly on any major matter they should ask for the advice of the church. So, with no elders, the work of a church still needs to move forward, and some temporary plan may be instituted as long as those doing some leading do not assume that they are elders even though they have not been appointed for that role. And they should do all they can to raise up men who can be elders.

What does the Bible tell us about the process of appointing elders? No specific details are given. Titus is told to see that elders are appointed in Crete, but Paul did not give instructions relative to the process. The best example we have of how a church appointed men to a special office is in Acts 6 where the apostles needed men to assist with caring for neglected widows. In Acts 6:3, the wording in most translations says that the people were to "choose" those whom the apostles would "appoint." The apostles gave the qualifications, involved the whole church in bringing forth names, and then the apostles "laid hands on them" to signify their appointment to the role.

To follow this plan in the selection of elders, the congregation would be instructed on the qualifications and be instructed to choose men whom the existing elders or, if no elders, an elder selection committee could appoint. This process might involve the following steps:

(1) the preacher would deliver one or two messages explaining the qualifications of elders;

(2) the members of the congregation would be asked to submit and sign forms, which list the qualifications from Paul's letters to Timothy

and Titus. Then the members would write on the form the names they wish to submit after checking that they meet each of the qualifications;

(3) a designated committee of existing elders or others appointed for the purpose would tabulate the submitted forms and make a list of those being mentioned most often and who, therefore, stand out above the others;

(4) the existing elders or, if not elders, a selection committee, would review these persons to see if they know of a reason why any on the list should be dropped because of something they know that disqualifies them, which the congregation generally would not know;

(5) the elders or selection committee would then decide how many from the list of those most often mentioned should be submitted to the congregation as proposed elders;

(6) the congregation should then be given the names and be told that if anyone has a scriptural objection to any of those on the list that person should submit a signed statement explaining why;

(7) the elders or committee should consider any such objections to see whether that should disqualify the person;

(8) the remaining candidates should then be presented to the congregation as those chosen by them and should be ordained in something like the "laying on of hands" as the apostles did.

This process uses what we know from Scripture about setting aside men as elders. The congregation is prepared; they have the opportunity to suggest names and, thus, to be involved in the process. An appropriate number from those mentioned most often by the congregation are chosen. The members are given an opportunity to submit a scriptural objection. Finally, then, the men are given the congregation's approval as elders.

Before presenting specifics about how the elders should operate, let's first look at nine principles of leadership that will appear at different times in the various chapters in this book. Since the elders provide the primary leadership in a congregation, they need to keep these principles in mind. But deacons, ministry directors, preachers, and others who lead in various aspects of the work of the church should be keeping these principles in mind as they do their activities.

(1) Dreaming expands possibilities.

(2) Planning promotes action.

(3) Involvement builds interest.

(4) Responsibility unlocks potential.

(5) Communication strengthens relationships.

(6) Sacrifice promotes commitment.

(7) Appreciation sparks effort.

(8) Training increases effectiveness.

(9) Evaluation improves performance.

Now let's move to specific thoughts about how the elders of a congregation can do their job well. An eldership should review this list to remind themselves of things they might wish to do to improve their work.

1. **Elders should meet regularly to govern the church well.** For these meetings to function effectively, someone needs to be chairman, and in most churches, the elders rotate the chairmanship monthly or, perhaps, every two or three months. It is best for no one elder to be chair for a longer period of time than this since that would tend to set him apart as having more authority than the others. All elders need an equal standing even though some may be more experienced than others.

2. **The elder chair should plan the meetings by the preparation of an agenda.** He can have another elder or two and perhaps a minister to help him in preparing a list of those things that need to be discussed in an upcoming meeting. Such a group could be called a Steering Committee, which would rotate elders on the committee and which would meet prior to each meeting. As they prepare an agenda, two questions should be asked about any item up for consideration.

    The first question is whether the matter can well be handled by an individual or committee working in a particular area. For example, if the matter deals with missions, can it best be referred to the Missions Committee, or if it deals with education, can it best be referred to the Education Committee? Matters should always be dealt with at the lowest possible level in the organization that is equipped to handle it. Often elders spend time caring for items that could best be dealt with by those closer to the situation. This plan of referral preserves the time of the elders for dealing with those matters that do require their attention.

A second question is whether sufficient study has been given to the matter before it is placed on the agenda. Elders often waste a large amount of time discussing a topic on which they are not sufficiently informed. So they talk about "What if" and finally determine to wait on any decision until they have more information. It is so much better if a matter is not presented for their discussion until all the necessary information has been gathered and perhaps even a couple of options for the solution can be ready for discussion. Maybe a person best informed on the situation can present the information to the elders or perhaps a committee in the area should review it first and write a recommendation. Matters on which sufficient information is not available to make a wise decision should not be on the agenda unless those making the decision just wish to get beginning input from various elders.

So the chairman, with whatever assistance he needs, should

(1) send matters to others if they can deal with it, and

(2) see that necessary information is ready to be presented to the elders when a matter is raised for consideration.

Of course, in developing the agenda, the chairman, after the routine matters, will place first those issues of greatest importance so they will be considered first. Having a printed agenda to distribute at the meeting is a good idea because those present will then see what items are to be discussed, and they will tend to adjust their comments on each issue according to the number of items to be covered.

Someone, of course, should be designated to keep careful minutes of the meeting so that any decisions made will be recorded and can be checked later should questions arise. If handouts about a matter are distributed, these can be attached to the minutes, so there will be a permanent copy for future reference. The minutes should be distributed to all elders before the next meeting, so they can have a chance to note anything that might not have been properly recorded.

3. **In their meetings, elders should give time to pray for specific people in the congregation.** One eldership I know about begins every meeting by asking each elder to mention things that should be included in their opening prayer. Sometimes individuals are mentioned who have an illness, family difficulties, or other needs, and this not only gets the situation mentioned in prayer, but also informs all the elders about that particular need. Other matters raised for the opening prayer may deal with works going on in various ministries. Thus, the elders can pray for people going on a mission trip, the young people going on a retreat, a decision a ministry is facing, or the preacher who is beginning a series on a crucial topic.

4. **Elders should delegate to others as much as possible.** The elders can, for example, create ministries for each area of work within the congregation: care of the building, worship, local evangelism, missions, youth, education, women's program, hospital visitation, seniors, fellowship, parenting, benevolence, communication, and others. Then they can appoint a deacon or other qualified person to lead in that area, but it is best if no elders serve as the chair of one of these areas. These chairpersons can all be assigned to be under a particular elder or small elder committee who can generally oversee that work and which would be the one to whom this chairperson would go first for advice or to report on the work. This elder or committee also would represent that work to the elders.

   This elder or small group of elders would meet periodically, perhaps quarterly, with this chair to keep up with the work in that area and occasionally the elder or committee would report to the full eldership things happening or get elder input on matters involving the ministry. The chair of that ministry would be told that he should bring to the overseeing elder or committee anything he believes needs approval of the elders. Then that elder or committee would decide what to handle himself and what needed to go on to the full eldership.

   This plan takes elders out of having to be the direct administrators of all areas of work in the church and gives them much more time to deal with the spiritual life of the congregation. This plan also better utilizes the talents of deacons and others who now lead at the ministry level. One of the most important works of an eldership is to utilize others to the fullest extent they can. Remember that since involvement builds interest, the more people who are involved in managing and carrying out various roles in the church, the more people who will be interested in the work the church is doing.

Involving others was the plan of the apostles in Acts 6 when they said we need to devote ourselves to the ministry of the Word and prayer, so they appointed qualified men to oversee the work of benevolence. Each eldership, then, should ask whether they are fully utilizing others and whether they have freed themselves of responsibilities they can give to someone else.

5. **Elders need to fulfill their responsibility to teach and guide individuals and to oversee the spiritual development of the members of the church.** Here are several suggestions about the work of elders in guiding individual members.

    a. Elders should be readily available to members. In some congregations, at least two elders are always available in the vestibule after the Sunday evening service so that anyone who wishes may request special prayers, ask any question, or raise any issue. In other congregations, an elder always leads the closing prayer on Sunday morning and informs the congregation that he will be available at the front afterward.

    b. Elders need to do regular visiting. No member should ever be in the hospital, for example, without receiving a visit from at least one elder. And at the passing of any member, elders should always visit the family and attend the funeral. One elder's wife always bakes a delicious lemon cake, which she and her husband take to the family of a member who has died. This act of kindness is not only appreciated, but it's also a tangible way to express sympathy and helps provide food for the family at a crucial time.

    Since elders are to be hospitable, they need to have members in their home. They may have a small group Bible study to achieve this or they may just occasionally have a few members to their home. These guests shouldn't just be their own friends, but should include people who may especially need fellowship like those who have lost a mate, those who have recently been baptized or placed membership or those whom the elder is advising on problems.

The elders need to have a way to know which members need their special attention. Their wives often hear of someone's troubles before they do, so these women can be a good source of information about who needs help. One congregation appoints an elder to be in each Sunday morning class from high school through all adult classes. This elder and his wife are present in that class each Sunday, which means they're meeting people and are available. In this way an elder knows who in his group is hurting spiritually and physically. He may occasionally teach the class, but his presence all the time shows an openness of the elders and helps him to know who needs his attention. The elder assigned to the high school class actually goes on high school retreats and on mission trips with the students. This not only allows him to oversee these works, but also gives the opportunity for the young people to know an elder personally and to be engaged with someone in another generation.

c. Another eldership goes through the directory of members at a meeting once a year and assigns an elder to visit in the home of each member during the next 12-month period. This means that every member/family gets a visit from an elder each year—just to be acquainted and to be open for questions. One of their objectives in this practice is to find out the extent to which each member is engaged not only in attendance, but also in Christian service. During the visit, they ask the member about their involvement. Those not sufficiently involved are asked what service they would be interested in doing, and then someone leading that area of work is asked to contact them.

d. Elders and deacons need to be working together well. In addition to being sure to have each deacon assigned to a beneficial work, elders can divide up the deacons among themselves and see that one of them takes each deacon out to lunch or in some other way has a visit each year with an elder. These sessions are for building personal relationships as well as discussing the deacon's service. Remember, communication strengthens relationships. Sometimes, when a major decision is in process, such as a new major building project or adding an additional minister or taking a special contribution, the elders would do well to have a meeting with the deacons to get their input. Not necessarily asking them for a vote on the matter, although they could, but at least involving them in the discussion. This will enable the deacons to help answer questions people may have and is more likely to draw better participation in the project from the deacons.

6. **The elders need to accept the responsibility for the spiritual growth of the members of the church.** To fulfill this role, they not only need to be sure that well-qualified people teach each class from pre-school through seniors, but they also need to agree on a list of the subjects on which their members need to be well-informed. Then the preacher and those who plan classes, even starting with pre-school and elementary students, should be aware of the topics on which the elders believe the members should be taught. In Acts 20:28-31, Paul urges the elders of the church in Ephesus to "Keep watch over the flock." He says "savage wolves" will enter the flock and try to draw them away into false teaching. Elders, then, must see that each member of the flock is well-informed, even deeply committed to the truth of God on many topics. Below is a list of objectives that could serve as a beginning point for a list an eldership can develop to share with their preaching minister and those planning topics for Bible classes. They would say to them that they are not asking that the pulpit and the classroom be limited to these items, but would like to be sure that each person, adult, and youth who has grown up in this church would be well-informed from the Scriptures on these topics. This list below can be used as a starting point for developing such a list. Would it not be excellent if every member could demonstrate that he or she could do each of the following things?

    a. Can explain the plan of salvation and encourage someone to obey it.
    b. Can state the case for the existence of God.
    c. Can state the case for the Bible as an infallible revelation inspired by God and as the authority for Christian faith and practice

d. Can use the principles of hermeneutics to determine the meaning of Bible passages.
e. Can state the case for the divinity of Christ.
f. Can explain the nature of the church as the saved, the body of Christ and that the church is not a denomination.
g. Can trace the predictions and the history of the departure from Christ's original plan for the church as revealed in the New Testament, the efforts of the Reformation Movement to move back in that direction, and then the efforts to restore the New Testament plan for the teaching and practice of the church.
h. Can provide reasons from Scripture as to why churches of Christ do not use instruments with their singing.
i. Can provide reasons from Scripture as to why in churches of Christ only men lead in worship.
j. Can use the Sermon on the Mount, the list of Christian graces, and the list of the fruits of the Spirit to describe Christ-like character and will demonstrate such qualities in his/her personal life.
k. Can trace the story of God's plan for saving sinful people starting with the sin of Adam through God's choice of Abraham to build a family, God's work through the nation of Israel both to provide a Messiah and to demonstrate that a person cannot keep the law to perfection, to the coming of Christ and His undeserved death, and finally the establishment of the church as the fulfillment of God's plan.
l. Can state the case for creation as opposed to evolution.
m. Can properly use helps for Bible study such as a concordance, Bible dictionary, commentaries, and the internet.
n. Can participate in worship in a meaningful and scriptural way.
o. Can tell how a Christian would respond to various situations involving moral decisions.
p. Can explain God's plan for marriage, divorce, and re-marriage.
q. Will use relationships with others such as neighbors or fellow-workers as opportunities to bring people to Christ.
r. Will submit to parents, elders, and others in positions of authority.

s. Will be regular in attendance at Sunday worship and Bible study times.

t. Will actively be engaged in serving such as helping others, working in church ministries, speaking with friends, and inviting them to attend or to have a Bible study.

There are many ways in which leaders can help the congregation to reach these objectives. When, for example, the educational director selects a particular book in the Bible for study, he should note some passages in that book that provide the basis for a study of one or more of these points and should see that teachers cover that objective well. Sometimes those planning classes should develop a series of lessons to cover some of these issues. When the preacher is planning his sermons, he should keep these objectives in mind and have sermons to deal with them. Even those planning the studies for children and teens can find ways to include these topics in a useful way. The elders, preacher, and educational director should remember that more than one lesson or one sermon on a topic is needed to get into a member's mind all he or she needs to know on one of these items. This means that over a period of time, several sermons and lessons should be presented on each of these topics.

7. **The elders need to be growing spiritually themselves.** One congregation has a plan that on every fifth Saturday, the elders meet to discuss a more difficult Bible question. They ask the ministers to gather with them, and they either bring in an outside person who is expert in that area or they assign someone from their own group to prepare information to share. Then they spend time in discussing the matter to get a better grip on that question. They deal with such topics as marriage, how the church should be caring for the poor, Christ's return and the end of the world, the Restoration Movement, and many other topics.

8. **The elders are responsible for the financial management of the church, but could use some people who are not elders to assist in this work.** Here are a few things that elders should ensure are happening relative to church finances:

a. regular teaching from Scripture about giving and one's use of money;
b. frequent expression of appreciation for what the congregation is giving;
c. careful accounting for all funds and involving more than one person in that process;
d. regular reporting to the congregation about what is being given and how it is being used;
e. involving those outside the eldership in helping to plan the budget;
f. "selling" the congregation on what important works the contribution will provide; and
g. encouraging giving throughout the year, not just at budget time.

9. **The elders should be especially good at expressing appreciation to members**. Remember, appreciation sparks effort. Sometimes this appreciation will be from the pulpit as elders thank members for their generosity or honor someone for service. Thanking people for what they are doing should also be part of what elders do individually for those with whom they work in various ministries. The full eldership should regularly ask people to come to their meeting to receive commendation for their work. Often elders do this when someone has decided to lay aside some work he has been doing for a long time, and that is fine. But if the elders had thanked the person more regularly for their work, then they might not have stepped out of that role so soon. One group of elders decided to spend part of their meeting time writing notes to people in the congregation who needed thanks. The chairman brought paper, envelopes, and a list of people serving in various roles, and the elders wrote notes of thanks. Some roles are so "behind the scenes" that no one knows much about them such as those preparing communion or those counting and depositing the money or someone who keeps up the flower beds. Elders should be good "thankers." And that would include expressing appreciation to preachers, church secretaries, and those who care for the building.

HOW THE ELDERS Can be Their Best

A SPECIAL NOTE ABOUT THANKING PEOPLE

In our time, some among us think those who follow the scriptural teaching about only men serving as elders and only men leading in the public worship are leaving women to be used only in unimportant roles. Some even leave the church for a place that gives women public roles of leadership because they believe women should have more important work to do. If we are to use the early church as our model, however, we will follow its teaching about the differing roles of men and of women, but there is something elders should do that will show the true importance of the work of women among us. DO MORE TO THANK WOMEN PUBLICLY FOR THE IMPORTANT WORK THEY DO. So, on a Sunday morning, thank all those who are teaching in pre-school and elementary classes—have them stand and offer a prayer of thanks and blessing for the vital work they do. Use a bulletin story to express thanks to women who serve in the nursery. Have a dinner to thank all teachers, and note those who teach at different age levels. Find appropriate ways to honor publicly those who teach in the women's program, who serve in prison ministry, who grade correspondence lessons, who serve in benevolence. There will certainly be women filling important roles in these ministries as well as in other ones. By giving public honor to those who serve in these ways, the work of women will be elevated, and people will see the importance of roles women fill among you. When someone comes to be baptized, tell how that person learned the truth, and often, that will be through the work of a woman. And, of course, do not forget to honor women who fill the role of wives and mothers and grandmothers, because there is no role more important than this. Mother's Day would be a good time for this.

Thanking those in such roles will demonstrate how important these roles are to the church and will help show that just because a person is not leading a song nor leading the prayer in the public worship does not mean that this person is not serving in a vitally important role.

10. **The elders should plan well for the coming year.** Remember, planning promotes action. Some churches begin in August or September to plan for the year starting in January. They ask each ministry to think about what they could do in the coming year and to plan what it would take for doing well what is already happening and what might be done additionally to meet their purpose. Then they ask each ministry to submit a plan for how these good things could happen and what financial and personnel support it would take. Based on this, the ministry submits a proposed budget. These proposals are then reviewed by a designated group. That group could be the elders, the deacons, or a meeting of all of those who have submitted proposals. One congregation has all those who submitted proposals to meet and discuss them all. Then this group looks at the giving for the current year and determines how much of an increase they should propose to the elders in light of the growth of the congregation and economic circumstances. Based on this information, the group sets a target increase for the coming year and then decides on what proposals can be implemented and which must wait for a later time. They then submit this information to the elders for their consideration.

Whatever the plan, it should begin early to allow for proper time for review. Then by early December, a projected budget should be announced to the congregation with appropriate information given and "selling" of the new items, which can be included if the contribution increases. Such a presentation can help people decide to increase their contributions. Then by mid-December, the members can be asked to submit "purpose cards" indicating what they expect to give. This process is important because if helps families to plan what they will give and thus they "purpose in their hearts" as says the Scripture in 2 Corinthians 9:7.

When someone privately adds up the amount promised by the cards, the elders can then decide how much to expect the contribution will be and how much of the proposed budget is reasonable to do. Typically, the contribution will be larger than the amount from the purpose cards because some will not submit a card. By using information from those who did budget planning, the current contribution, the purpose cards, and the actual contributions during January, the elders can have a good indication of what the contribution will be during the coming year and can proceed accordingly. So, they should begin the process early enough for these various steps to be completed.

11. **Sometimes elders need to take an even longer view of things than just the coming year.** Remember, dreaming expands possibilities. It would be helpful if they had a five-year plan with some overarching goals and specific items to be achieved during that time. For such planning, they may want to bring in someone who specializes in long-range planning for churches. Or they may want to ask each ministry to look ahead over the next five years and provide a report to a group (maybe with representation from the elders, ministers, teachers, deacons, and others) that will review the ideas submitted and build a common long-range plan from these reports. Each year, this group should review the progress and report to the elders.

12. **The elders should recognize that training increases effectiveness.** That means that they are constantly providing training for those in various roles. They train the deacons. They provide opportunities for ministers to go to training seminars or lectureships. They find ways to provide training within the congregation for the roles that members play, such as training them to know how to reach out to others to serve them and to bring them to church with them. Those who teach from the youngest to the oldest need opportunities for training. Some congregations bring people to their church to train teachers, and others send them to places where they can learn more about what they are doing. So, elders should look at each role being filled in the congregation and ask how training might help that person to do better and then provide such training.

13. **Elders should have a plan to evaluate each employee and each ministry because evaluation improves performance.** Once a year, each minister should be asked to evaluate his own work and how he plans to make improvements. He could submit this report to the elders for their review, and the elders could meet with the minister in an open discussion of his report with the elders asking questions and giving statements of support.

As each ministry prepares its budget, it should be asked to set its goals for the coming year and then when that planning time of the year comes around again, they should be asked to evaluate how they did on their goals for the past year and set goals for the coming year.

Periodically, the elders could evaluate their own work. They could ask such questions as these:

- Are we being efficient in our work?
- Are we working enough with our members on a personal basis?
- Are we being open enough with the church, while protecting what needs to be private? Could we do more to give our members confidence in the leadership?
- What ministries in our congregation need to be strengthened?
- Are we utilizing our deacons well?
- Are our education program and our pulpit helping sufficiently in reaching the goals we have set for what the congregation needs to know and do?

Make a list of any other questions that should also be asked.

14. **Finally a comment about the relationship between elders and preachers.** Often preachers leave a church or even the ministry because they feel they have been burned by an eldership that did not show appreciation for their work or did not show understanding for the load the preacher was carrying. It is good to have the minister present for elders' meetings, so he will better understand what is happening and will not feel excluded. Of course there are times when the elders are discussing matters intended for elders only, but most of the time the minister can learn from and contribute to the meeting. Many elderships suggest that a minister take a week off to plan for the coming year of sermons and, in addition, good vacation time is needed. Elders should review the minister's salary annually to provide occasional salary and benefit increases, and they should look for various ways of expressing appreciation. Elders should certainly find ways to build the relationship with its ministers.

This chapter seeks to give elders ideas about how they might take steps forward in their work. It will help any eldership to walk through these suggestions and select a few that would be most helpful for them. Consider having a meeting on a Saturday morning in which all the elders review this chapter as a group and ask what they might learn from these ideas to make improvements in their work. A year later, they might do the same with a review of what they hoped to do and a projection of more ways they might improve.

The work of elders is key to the progress of a local congregation. Christ knew this when He devised the plan for each church to have a qualified group of men to serve in this role. So, those serving in this vital way need to be asking, "How can we fill this role in a better way?"

CHAPTER 3

THE DEACONS AND MINISTRY DIRECTORS

Can be Their Best

Along with directing that each congregation should have elders to lead, the New Testament also teaches that each congregation should have deacons to serve. The word *deacon* is just the English spelling of the Greek word *diakonos*, which means "to serve." To paraphrase Matthew 20:28, Jesus said that He did not come to be "deaconed to" but "to deacon." First Timothy 3 gives the qualifications for a deacon, but does not give details about what they are to do.

Although the term *deacon* is used in the New Testament to refer to these specific men who are to be appointed as servants in the church, it is also sometimes used in a more general sense. Everyone in the church is to be a servant (2 Corinthians 4:5), and it is in this more general sense that Phoebe is called a servant of the church in Romans 16:1-2.

It is clear from Acts 6 that church leaders need helpers. The word *deacon* is not used there, but clearly the apostles needed a second level of leadership to care for the distribution of food to the poor Grecian widows.

And so it is in the church. The elders need men whom the congregation has set apart whom they can use for various responsibilities that need to be met. In turn, such delegation will allow the elders the time to be counselors, managers, and shepherds. Without being able to use others for many things that need to be done, the elders will get bogged down in details, which will keep them from doing their best at what should be their work.

Deacons, then, are men in whom the congregation has expressed confidence and, thus, to whom the elders may delegate various tasks. Though elders certainly can delegate work to others, both to men and to women, having a core of men in whom the congregation has expressed their trust is helpful for many good works.

Sometimes the work of a deacon will be to lead in an area of work, like being in charge of the education ministry or of the building upkeep. The elders may also need men to whom they can delegate a work to be done that is not leading others. A deacon, for example, might be given the responsibility for preparing the communion each Sunday or for opening the building 30 minutes before each service. These are roles requiring responsibility and might be the work of a deacon.

The Bible does not, however, say that the only ones to whom the elders delegate responsibilities must be deacons. The elders, for example, might choose a woman to lead the women's ministry and might choose a man who is not a deacon, but is trained in accounting to chair the finance committee. The leader of an area of work might be called chairman of a committee or the ministry director for a particular work. The Bible speaks of such serving when it says in Romans 12:8 that one who "leads" should lead with diligence.

What, then, are some suggestions for the work of those who fill the role of a deacon or ministry director as they lead?

1. One leading in a work should know **to whom he is to report** and how often he is supposed to share with that person or overseeing committee a report about his work. For this relationship to work well, he should keep that person or group well informed about his work, through occasional meetings and sometimes through a monthly or quarterly email.

2. One leading in a work should **know exactly what his responsibilities are**. If there is any uncertainty, he should ask, maybe even asking for something in writing. Failures in leadership are often due to a person's not understanding clearly what his responsibilities are. For example, is the worship leader responsible for seeing that someone is greeting at the door or does that fall to the one overseeing local outreach? Or to take another case, who is responsible for keeping useful and timely

information on the bulletin boards in the church? Does that fall to the preacher or to building and grounds or to worship or to evangelism? One who is given a leadership responsibility, then, needs to be sure exactly what the responsibilities are and are not. Clarity on this point will keep the leader from ever having to say, "I didn't know that was my responsibility."

3. One leading in a work should have **a good annual plan** for his work. In August or September of each year (assuming a fiscal-year start in January), the leader should begin the planning process for the coming year. By that time, the elders should have set goals and broad plans for the coming year. On the basis of these plans, each leader, along with his committee if he uses one, will lay out specific objectives for the year. Some of these objectives may be the same each year, but others may be special goals that fit that particular year. So, if he is in charge of the building committee, he may have as a continuing goal that, "The building will always be in a condition to be conducive to worship and study." As ways of carrying out this broad goal, there may be specific actions to take such as, "The building will be clean and at the proper temperature each time the building is used." But in a particular year, he may plan a specific action such as "The classrooms will be repainted" or "The lighting on the podium will be improved." Such planning will allow him to include requests for the coming year's budget as it is being prepared.

4. The one leading in a work should have **clear information about the financial responsibilities** he has. How much money has been allotted to his work? What reports should he submit? What authority does he have to spend or in what cases does he need to get permission? In one church, for example, the deacon in charge of disaster relief has a fund from which to work. He was given permission to spend up to $3,000 on his own authority, but for amounts above that, he needed to get permission from his supervising committee composed of an elder and four others. The reason for this arrangement was that when he took a group to help in a disaster, he might run into matters that required quick action and for him to have to get permission for everything he spent through a committee would have hampered his work. On the

other hand, however, to protect him from someone who might think he was not spending the money wisely, for larger amounts he would have the backing of a supervising committee. A leader of a work, then, needs to be clear on how much he can spend and the process he should follow in doing so.

5. One leading in a work should **have appropriate help in carrying out his work.** The Mission Committee, for example, may have a specific member responsible for communicating with and representing the needs of each different missionary whom the church helps. Though the Missions Committee, as a whole, works out the broader plan for the year and the expenditure for various works, this designated person keeps in touch with a specific missionary and represents him in discussions of missions about plans and expenditures. The leader responsible for education, to take another example, will likely have a person responsible for children's classes, youth classes, and adult classes. A third case is the leader in local evangelism who may have someone responsible for greeting and follow-up with visitors, another who is in charge of home Bible studies, and someone else who works with suggesting and developing special events that the church should be having. Just as the elders, then, need those to whom they can assign work, the leaders of specific areas will likely need those who help them carry out their work.

6. The leaders of various works need **regular contact with the elder or elders who oversee their work.** In some cases each elder may have two or three of the ministries of the church for which he has oversight or the plan may be to have a committee of two or three elders to oversee various works. Whatever the plan, it should include periodic contact between the leader and his elder oversight. Maybe this will be a meeting each quarter in which the ministry directors report on what is happening in their work, ask questions on matters they are facing, convey information on problems they may be having, or review their budget status and financial needs, and refresh the elders on who is at work in their area and what they do. Such meetings keep lines of communication open and help elders to stay informed on the work of this particular area. Communication strengthens relationships. If

the elders don't set up such occasions with regularity, then the leader should ask for such meetings.

7. The leader of a ministry should **often provide praise for those in his area**. Appreciation sparks effort. He should drop notes of thanks, share praise when his committee meets, and even sometimes should ask for the elders to thank someone who has done especially well. He may want to take his group to breakfast, lunch, or dinner and use the occasion to thank them for their work. I know, for example, of a deacon who recently invited his overseeing elders and a few others to a dinner for a man who had been working in his ministry for 10 years. While at the dinner, he spoke words of appreciation for the work this man had done. This man will never forget this occasion. In Romans 16, Paul mentions a long list of those who had been his helpers, often telling what they had done to help him. What a great example to us of how to thank our fellow workers! (As I am writing this chapter, my wife just suggested that we have a worker who has done especially well in a ministry along with the deacon who leads that area and the other three elders and wives on the overseeing committee to our home for a meal before the worker and his wife leave to move elsewhere. Fits neatly with this item on the list.)

8. The leader of an area should **be open to suggestions from those working with him**. At their regular meetings and in his personal contact with his fellow workers, he should be open to suggestions. He should be a good listener. Communication strengthens relationships. Often those working in one aspect of his responsibilities may be using a practice that could be used in other areas of the work. Sometimes a leader wants to use his position of leadership to oversee, but is not open to suggestions. A sense of openness will not only allow for improvements in the work, but will also give those working with him a greater sense of satisfaction in their relationship with him.

9. The leader of a ministry should **help keep the congregation informed** on what is happening in his area. By using the bulletin, the church email list, and public announcements, the director of an area should let people know of coming events, of help he will need, and of successes

his area has experienced. Thus, when the teens have had a good retreat, the congregation should know about it. When the education committee has the classes planned for the fall quarter, the congregation needs to be well-informed about what is coming and why it is important. When there have been important successes by a missionary the congregation supports, that information should be shared. When the prison ministry has baptisms, the church should know about it. Such information is helpful to the congregation in knowing that they are involved in doing good things, and it also helps them to know their money is being well spent. When new workers are needed in that area, the congregation will know that this area has been productive. So, the leader should use the methods available to him to keep the congregation informed on his area or work.

Deacons and ministry directors should look carefully over this list to see if there are areas in which they could improve in their leading. Write down items that would be good to do, and find ways to move before the good thought is lost.

CHAPTER 4

HOW THE PREACHER'S WORK
Can be its Best

The New Testament frequently mentions the work of the preacher. Acts records the very words of sermons—one from Stephen, three from Peter, and six from Paul. Thus, preaching was an extremely important part of the work of the early church. Paul instructs Timothy to "Preach the Word" and gives him great advice about how to get the message out. Paul also mentions the "evangelist" in his list of important roles in the church. If we, then, are to follow the pattern of the early church, we also must have effective preaching. Though learning in smaller groups is certainly important, there is also something special about learning and being encouraged in large groups, which has a special place in the work of the church. There is power in the pulpit because the preacher can interpret Scripture, make applications to daily living, and then persuade members to put these applications into practice.

Paul told the Corinthians that the instruction given by prophets and those who spoke in tongues were important parts of the worship (1 Corinthians 14). And speaking guided by the Holy Spirit through the Word is still vital to the health and growth of a congregation.

This chapter does not provide detailed instructions about how to prepare sermons, but seeks rather to give suggestions that can be helpful in the broader sense of the work of the minister. A preacher who wants to improve his service should review the items below and make a list of specific things to do.

HOW THE PREACHER'S WORK *Can be its Best*

1. **The preacher should have a broad list of topics to use, so he can be sure his preaching is covering the subjects about which his members need to be well-informed.** There is such a list in this book in the chapter on elders and a different list in my book called *Preaching: Man and Method* available from 21st Century Christian (Call 800.251.2477, or order online at *21stcc.com*). It is easy for a preacher to deliver excellent and scriptural sermons, but fail to cover topics on which his congregation should be well-informed. Every member of the church, for example, needs to be able to tell someone how to be saved. Do his sermons over the span of a year or two make a strong contribution to help members reach that goal? As another example, Christians, older and especially the young, need to be well informed and committed to the teaching of the New Testament on marriage, divorce, and re-marriage. Because we may not all agree on how to handle difficult cases, many preachers do not teach on what is clear on this key topic and, therefore, leave members poorly informed on this important matter.

    The preacher should be working with those who plan the topics for classes, so they can coordinate their efforts to cover the subjects on which the members need to be taught.

    Included in his list of topics should be sermons that teach why churches of Christ are different from denominational churches:

    (1) we seek to follow the model of the New Testament church in both doctrine and in practice,

    (2) we have elder-led churches,

    (3) our churches are autonomous,

    (4) we worship like the New Testament church did, including weekly communion and *a cappella* singing, and

    (5) we baptize for the forgiveness of sins and to put those baptized into Christ and His church.

    So, a preacher needs to develop a list of Bible topics on which his congregation needs to be clearly taught. Then, in planning his sermons, he should use a balanced approach, which will both inform and persuade the congregation on what the Lord wants them to know and do. He must also realize that new people are coming in, children are growing up, and older ones are forgetting. So onto that end, a single sermon on a needed topic every five years will not accomplish what needs to be done.

2. **A preacher needs to realize that his work from the pulpit is not just to inform, but it should also inspire and actuate.** He needs to excite people about the gospel and move them to action. One of the special features of speaking to a larger group is that it lends itself to being a time to stir the congregation to action. Think, for example, of how those running for office want to gather large crowds whom they can excite. If done properly, then, the preacher can strengthen the congregation's resolve to live and to serve as the Lord has called us to do.

3. **A preacher must establish strong ties with members.** If they like him personally, they are much more likely to listen well to his sermons. To achieve this goal, he must be available to them. He should have them into his home. He should have coffee with the guys. He should visit them in their homes. He should visit the sick in the hospital. I know of a preacher, for example, who attended the graveside service for the mother of a member, and that member, over a period of several years, continued to tell the preacher how much it meant for him to be there. When this preacher teaches and preaches, that member is ready to listen.

Since sports is a big thing with so many, a preacher can use sports as a tool. He can attend games in which members and their children are involved. He can play golf with members. He can keep up with teams that his members are following. He can use sports examples in sermons. If he is connected with sports, he seems like a regular guy, and the members like that.

Once a preacher decided he did not want members to feel they had to say anything to him after the sermon, so he slipped out the back door after the invitation song. It was not long before the elders asked him to move on because the members did not feel close to him.

So, every preacher should ask whether he is doing all he can to build strong ties with the members. In smaller congregations, the preacher should know every member by name. In larger churches, that may not be possible, but he should learn about as many people as possible.

4. **The preacher should live what he preaches.** When he speaks about kindness, the members should be thinking that he is kind, so he's qualified to speak on that topic. They recognize that he is kind to his family, his assistant, the elders, the widows, his family, and all the members. This conduct will make his sermon much stronger. And so it is with all subjects. His life must match his preaching. A preacher should make an inventory of his life. He should make a list of the qualities he preaches about from Galatians 5 and 2 Peter 2 and ask on which ones he should make a plan for improvement. He needs to be growing in the grace and knowledge of Christ.

5. **Preachers should work well with the elders.** The minister should have frequent contact with them in friendly situations. He can have coffee with them, play golf with them, go out for meals with them, and have them to his house for a meal. He should make a strong effort to make friends with them.

When he has proposals to make about the work of the church, he should work carefully. For starters, he should never surprise the elders. If anyone brings a request for which the proper groundwork has not been laid, the proposal is likely to be rejected. So when he has a plan, he should first mention to the elders that there is a problem or a need that should be addressed. Thus, he opens the door to thought about this need. Then he can volunteer to take a proposal to the elders. He can form a committee of three or four to work on developing the plan, and he can assign an elder to the committee. He may want to give a progress report as the plan moves forward. As the proposal is in its final stages, he can meet privately with a couple of elders to bring them on board. When the committee is finished with the report, the preacher and others on the committee can present the proposal. Because the elders have been expecting a plan about a need they have recognized, and some or all of them have had a look in advance at the proposal and have had a chance to make suggestions, their mindset tips toward acceptance when the proposal is made. Often a preacher works hard by himself on a plan and has high hopes, but then the elders reject the plan. This action becomes a barrier that may lead the preacher to decide to leave. If the minister will follow the plan above for developing an idea, he is much more likely to have his proposals accepted.

6. **The preacher must be extremely careful to avoid the appearance of evil in his connection with women.** If he is alone in his office and a woman comes to see him, he must leave the office door open, and he should not meet with her for long with no one else around. He should have a small window with glass in his door so that he is never completely out of sight. When he goes to visit women who live alone, he must always take his wife or someone else with him. He should not get in the car with a woman to drive her somewhere without another person in the car. There are two reasons for taking such care. The first is that he must never be in any situation that could give rise to questions or talk or criticism. Second, he must never be in a situation that would present a temptation to engage in anything immoral. Many good preachers have ruined their careers and hurt the church because they got involved with a woman starting from a circumstance that seemed innocent enough. So a preacher MUST stay out of any and all circumstances that could raise questions or lead to something sinful.

7. **A preacher should have a day off each week.** Since Sunday is a day of work for the preacher, the elders should give him a weekday to have time off. He can use this day to have time with his wife and family, to engage in recreational activity, or to read, but he is away from his normal work. Such time will reduce stress and make his working time more profitable. It will also make it more likely that the preacher will not suffer burn-out. There is a sense in which the preacher is on call 24 hours a day. He may get a call in the middle of the night about a member who has been in an accident or about a death, requiring him to be with the family. This sense of being constantly on call is all the more reason that he should be able to plan for a day off during the week. Many elderships offer resources for continuing education, a work fund that covers the cost of attending workshops and lectureships, and allows for the purchase of books. If this is not in a current plan the preacher has with the church, he might suggest such a fund the next time he discusses salary.

The minister should also have some time for vacation each year to do special things with his family. And many congregations, in addition, give a preacher a few days off in the summer to plan his sermons for the coming year. This is not time off but is, rather, an opportunity to work hard to determine the topics on which he will preach for the months ahead. Such planning makes it more likely that the preacher will include the subjects he should address and that he will do better sermon preparation because of knowing well in advance the topics he will use and when.

8. **The preacher should always be having at least one Bible study with a non-member.** He will be preaching that members should be finding people with whom they can study and bring to Christ, and he must set the example. He may be making the initial contact himself, or people may be bringing their contacts to him for study, but he should always have a study going. I know of a preacher in a relatively small town who had as many as 15 studies a week. He gave such studies a high priority. If this preacher could have so many, surely it is possible for other ministers to have at least one. Such studies will not only bring people to Christ and set a good example, but they will also give the preacher insight into topics about which he needs to preach. The minister may also be involved in a small group, which meets regularly to study Bible topics.

9. **When delivering his sermons, the preacher should establish a strong relationship with the audience.** The choice of the topic and his introduction to the sermon should help him develop that relationship because a congregation can recognize that the sermon will help them know something useful and important. He also establishes this strong bond by looking directly at people in the audience most of the time during the sermon. If he writes out his sermon, he must know it well enough to lift his eyes off the text to have eye contact with the audience. He should also occasionally move from behind the pulpit as he makes an important point so that the audience senses that he is speaking directly to them. And as he finishes making a point with this directness, he should drive the point hard to the end by not letting

his voice drop in volume or his eyes move from looking directly at them until he has finished the climactic sentence.

10. **The weakest point in most sermons is application.** An old story is told about an elder who posted a sign in huge letters on the back wall of the auditorium. It read "So What?" He was encouraging the preacher to make a good application of the sermon to daily life. In addition to explaining applications of Scripture regarding what we do or should do at work or play or home or school or in our cars while driving, the preacher should also illustrate the application to make it easier to remember.

    He may use an analogy, such as telling about a courageous Olympic athlete to urge us to have the courage to invite a friend to church. The second way to illustrate the application is to use a negative example. Thus the preacher could tell about someone who kept waiting to invite a friend to church, but suddenly that friend was killed in a car wreck. Think of how sad the Christian would feel in this situation. The strongest way to make an application stick is by using a positive example. In this case the preacher tells of a member of the church who invited a friend and that began the process of a Bible study followed by baptism and the great joy the Christian had in seeing his friend baptized. Such examples are best if they actually happened. If, however, the preacher cannot find true stories, then he can make up the story and tell the congregation—"It would be like this. Suppose —."

    By whatever means he does it, good sermons must include good applications. These are more likely to bring a positive response in the lives of those who hear him than just to explain a passage. As he looks over the content of what he plans to preach, the preacher should ask the question, "How many examples of application do I have and what type are they?" If he does not have enough or is not using enough positive cases, then he should work more on the sermon before he delivers it.

11. **Preachers need confidants.** Maybe he talks about a sermon he is working on with his wife. Or maybe he visits about his preaching with an elder-friend or a retired preacher in his church or a preacher in a nearby church, or by phone to someone far away. His conversations

about his preaching will help him to think of useful ideas on his own as well as getting sound advice from the other person. He may need to let off steam with someone who will listen and help him cool off. He may need to talk through a point of a sermon to get help on how to express it or to find good applications. Or he may need to talk through a problem at church with someone who is not part of the situation. Regardless, all preachers need someone to talk to.

So, occasionally a preacher will benefit from slowly reading through the above items and making a list of specific things he could do to improve his work as a minister. The work of preaching and helping people with spiritual needs outside of the pulpit is of vital importance to the church, and it is a rewarding challenge when done well.

CHAPTER 5

 **THE BIBLE SCHOOL PROGRAM** *Can be its Best*

In Matthew 28:28-29, Jesus says that His followers are to go to all nations to make disciples, to baptize, and then to teach what He has taught. Note this charge carefully. Jesus says to go and "make disciples." A *disciple* may be defined as "a learner." So we are to go and make learners. How does one "make learners?" He teaches. Having taught, we are to "baptize." And having baptized, we are to be "teaching them" what Jesus has taught. Put more simply, we are to teach, baptize, and teach again.

In Acts 1:8, Jesus gives this charge in a different way, but with the same basic meaning. He told the apostles they were to go into Jerusalem, Judea, Samaria, and to the end of the earth being "His witnesses." Why does one "witness?" To help people to learn. And in Acts 2, Peter carries out this command by preaching a great sermon in which he witnesses and teaches. He gives three reasons why his audience should believe in Jesus: He worked miracles, He fulfilled prophecy, and He was raised from the dead. So, Peter concludes, "God has made Him both Lord and Christ, this Jesus whom you crucified" (Acts 2:36). Now he has made disciples (learners) who ask "What shall we do?" To which Peter replies that they should "Be baptized for the forgiveness of your sins." So now we see the making of disciples and baptizing, so what comes next? "They continued steadfastly in the apostles' teaching (Acts 2:42). So, Jesus said to teach, baptize, and teach, they followed exactly what he said.

Now, we come to today. We should be doing the same thing. Every church must be a teaching church. So, like Peter, the preacher is teaching the whole congregation. But we need other opportunities to teach, which will be adapted to the more specific needs of various ages and circumstances.

We must constantly be teaching the fundamentals of the faith. Many who leave the church do so because they are not clear on the essentials of the faith. For all they have been taught, one church is as good as another. So those planning the curriculum, particularly for the younger ages, should find effective and interesting ways to teach the basics of the faith. We should help parents with their teaching of children and teens. And we need to teach people how to teach others.

In designing the education program to help with such needs, we can supplement what the preacher does in his proclamation. His sermons should call people to action. Through our classes, however, we can meet more specific spiritual needs of various groups and situations.

Most churches have chosen to have classes on Sunday morning when members are gathered for the Sunday services and to have classes some night during the week, usually on Wednesday. In addition, some have small groups for Bible study and fellowship. And what are these study opportunities to achieve? In the chapter on elders is a list of learning objectives, which the elders should use to guide their shepherding of the church. That list is repeated here to help those seeking to meet the needs of various groups through teaching classes.

a. Can explain the plan of salvation and encourage someone to obey it.

b. Can state the case for the existence of God.

c. Can state the case for the Bible as an infallible revelation inspired by God and as the authority for Christian faith and practice

d. Can use the principles of hermeneutics to determine the meaning of Bible passages.

e. Can state the case for the divinity of Christ.

f. Can explain the nature of the church as the saved, the body of Christ and that the church is not a denomination.

g. Can trace the predictions and the history of the departure from Christ's original plan for the church as revealed in the New Testament, the efforts of the Reformation Movement to move back in that direction, and then the efforts to restore the New Testament plan for the teaching and practice of the church.

h. Can provide reasons from Scripture as to why churches of Christ do not use instruments with their singing.
i. Can provide reasons from Scripture as to why in churches of Christ only men lead in worship.
j. Can use the Sermon on the Mount, the list of Christian graces, and the list of the fruits of the Spirit to describe Christ-like character and will demonstrate such qualities in his/her personal life.
k. Can trace the story of God's plan for saving sinful people starting with the sin of Adam through God's choice of Abraham to build a family, God's work through the nation of Israel both to provide a Messiah and to demonstrate that a person cannot keep the law to perfection, to the coming of Christ and His undeserved death, and finally the establishment of the church as the fulfillment of God's plan.
l. Can state the case for creation as opposed to evolution.
m. Can properly use helps for Bible study such as a concordance, Bible dictionary, commentaries, and the internet.
n. Can participate in worship in a meaningful and scriptural way.
o. Can tell how a Christian would respond to various situations involving moral decisions.
p. Can explain God's plan for marriage, divorce, and re-marriage.
q. Will use relationships with others such as neighbors or fellow-workers as opportunities to bring people to Christ.
r. Will submit to parents, elders, and others in positions of authority.
s. Will be regular in attendance at Sunday worship and Bible study times.
t. Will actively be engaged in serving such as helping others, working in church ministries, speaking with friends, and inviting them to attend or to have a Bible study.

Following are suggestions for those planning the educational program of the congregation's classes and for those who are teaching the classes. These suggestions should be reviewed periodically to see what improvements could be made in the education program.

1. **All classes, from the youngest to the oldest and on Sunday and Wednesday, should be designed to achieve the objectives stated above.** The classes should, of course, involve other objectives and topics, but those in charge should be sure these listed items are being covered over a period of time. To take just one example, consider the objective that every member should be able to explain the plan of salvation to someone. Surely we would want our congregation to achieve this objective. But how do we go about achieving it? We start teaching the plan in classes for elementary school students and to high school students. We teach it in adult classes. And the minister preaches about it. We not only teach about it, but we practice how to share it with others. To do this we could have Wednesday night classes in which members role play teaching the plan of salvation to a neighbor or fellow worker. We know that being sure each member can tell the story of salvation is not a one-time thing. A sermon once every two years on baptism is not enough. There must be repetition in various forms. New people are coming in. Children are growing up. And people forget.

   So, those planning classes should look at these objectives frequently and determine a strategy for how they will help those attending to reach each of them. At what age level should the teaching about a particular objective begin? When the class is studying Matthew, which objectives should be included? When studying Acts or Genesis, which objectives should be included? What topical classes are needed to enable the congregation to be making good progress toward the objectives?

2. **Classes should include the "So What?"** Too frequently the application of Scripture is not included in teaching a class. Many adult classes, for example, study a passage of Scripture, but do not provide time for those in the class to consider how the passage should affect their lives on Monday morning.

   The class may, for example, study the passage in James 1:27, which says, "to visit orphans and widows in their affliction." The class might discuss who is an orphan and who is a widow and then may talk about how churches generally should seek to care for orphans and widows.

Maybe someone, for example, will tell about how orphan homes are in the budget. But the class should spend some time discussing how individual members of the class can help care for an orphan and how can they support widows. A couple, for example, might learn from the class about fostering a child. Class members might be encouraged to invite widows and widowers to eat with them when they go out on Sunday after church. Someone might tell about going to a home for the elderly and reading the Scriptures to an elderly person to show interest in them and to bring them comfort and instruction. A couple of families might take their children to such a home where an old acquaintance lives and sing some songs for her. Let the class come up with applications. Plans might even be made in the class for how a group could care for widows. Maybe the class plans a dinner for the widows and widowers in the congregation, which the elders and wives would attend. The class could provide and serve the food, and everyone would have a good time of fellowship, which those living alone truly need.

Even in children's classes it is also important to make the application. When studying about how children should demonstrate love, the children should be asked how they can show love to parents, to their own siblings, to classmates, and to those who need particular attention such as children in one-parent homes or children with special needs.

The weak point in many classes in Bible school is in stimulating the students to decide on something they will do to carry out the teaching of the Scripture they are studying. Time in each class session should be allotted for this purpose, and teachers should be taught how to evoke comments from those in the class about such applications. They may even ask in a class about applications of the previous week's lesson that the students used in their own lives. And such discussions will encourage others to make applications in their own lives.

3. **Classes should teach how to interpret Scripture.** As classes move through passages of Scripture, they should not only discuss the meaning of the passage, but should also discuss the principles to follow in interpreting a passage. They should, for example, study

how to use the context, how to find word meanings, how to use other passages on the same topic, and how to determine who said it and to whom and under what circumstances. We cannot teach our students what all Bible passages mean, but we can teach them how to examine a passage to determine what it meant to those who first received it and then how to apply it to their own situation. Teachers, then, should frequently identify to their students the principles to use for interpreting the Scriptures and show how to use these principles when studying a particular passage.

4. **We should involve the students as much as possible in the learning process.** So, students should be asked questions about the meaning and the application of a passage or topic under consideration. They should also be free to ask questions of the teacher, thus raising important questions, and the teacher should listen carefully. If the number of students in the class and the circumstances allow for it, there should be some group discussion. Maybe the topic or passage could be introduced, and then the class could be divided into groups of six or eight to discuss questions about the topic or passage. The more students are involved in the study, the more likely they are to remember what the Bible teaches about a topic or passage. This involvement will, of course, need to be suited to the age of those in the class, but such involvement should begin even in pre-school classes.

5. **Homework can be quite helpful.** Children's classes can send assignments home for parents to use with their children so they can show (and review) what they learned in the class. High school and adult classes can also have homework, which involves passages to read in advance or even questions to complete before class time. One teacher likes to use this combination. He uses worksheets for the students to complete during the class period. Then he asks the students to study their worksheet prior to the next class period. Then he gives a "written review" (he never calls it a test, of course) as the class assembles in which students complete a question sheet about the previous lesson. Then he spends the first few minutes of class time reviewing the answers to the questions, which lets those

who have participated in the homework see how well they did. It's also helpful to those who didn't complete it at all.

6. **If you use a book or material prepared from someone outside the church, be sure it is screened carefully to determine whether there are conclusions or comments that are not in harmony with the Scriptures.** If there are good materials on the topic you wish to study prepared by members of the church, these should be given preference. If materials written by those who do not share our beliefs are taught unchecked, members of the class will get a wrong impression of what the Bible teaches. One way to deal with such content is to put a statement from the book before the class and let them discuss whether or not it is scriptural.

7. **Teachers should be encouraged to use visuals when possible.** There may be videos available from a good teacher on the subject, which teachers can show and which can provide time for questions and discussion afterward. The teachers can use PowerPoint, a handout, worksheets, or write on a board to enable students to use their eyes as well as their ears. Children's classes, of course, should use visuals and hand work appropriate for the age and topic.

8. **If several classes are studying the same topic, a help session for teachers can be useful.** Before the quarter begins, some congregations conduct prep sessions for teachers of pre-school or elementary classes that are doing similar lessons. These sessions review the basic content, discuss methods, and indicate the help available in the materials room. One congregation assigns most adult classes the same topic and then provides a Wednesday night class for the teachers of these Sunday morning classes to provide an outline with the information needed for the Sunday morning class session and an opportunity for these teachers to discuss the subject as part of their preparation, which leads to the next point.

9. **Students need to be given an opportunity to demonstrate what they have learned.** In school, whether elementary, high school, or college, teachers would never feel they had done their job if there were no opportunity to see what students had learned. Just to make the

point, suppose a teacher gave a college class their outside reading list, but explained that the students would not have any questions on the test over that material nor would they have any opportunity to show whether they had read those assignments. How many would do the reading? Similarly, how many students in our church adult classes are ever asked to show what they have learned? No wonder we have so many adults who have gone to class for years who could not show a person the plan of salvation!

Teachers and those who plan the teaching should suggest ways students can demonstrate what they have learned. This may be by oral questions at the beginning of the class that review the previous week's lesson or it may be through a few written questions for class members regarding that material. Teachers might also use role playing to give people a chance to show the application of what they have learned. One church had an adult and a teen class studying the same topic on Wednesday nights. As they started each night's lesson, they gave a quiz over the previous lesson and then determined the average score. The adult class and high school class were in competition with each other and had fun in comparing the scores. In the same way, teachers could use some form of evaluation to let students show what they have learned. Knowing that such evaluation will be used helps students to learn more.

10. **Every class, from nursery to older adults, to women's classes and men's classes should be taught to treat visitors in special ways.** Often visitors with small children decide whether to return on the quality of the nursery. Good children's classes also have a special attraction. And in high school and adult classes, the people should be taught to welcome visitors and even to follow up with a call, note, or visit to let them know they are welcome and are encouraged to return. Even if some other group has a follow-up plan, the class should do that as well.

11. **For adult classes, some churches have a class chairman, a different role than that of the teacher.** This class chair often helps in selecting the teacher for the class and arranges for class fellowship times such as monthly or quarterly gatherings for fun and fellowship. The chair

also sees that there is an up-to-date class role, and that those who are absent receive a call or visit or card. Having such a person takes a load from the teacher, allowing him/her to focus on the lesson to be taught.

12. **Those who are going to teach for a quarter or other period of time should be chosen well enough in advance to allow them to make good preparation.** If, for example, someone is going to teach an adult class which is not his own regular class, he would do well to attend the class for a few sessions before he becomes the teacher. This will give him a chance to meet some of the people and to get the feel of how the class likes to operate. Sufficient time also gives the teacher, whether teaching pre-school or adult, an opportunity to study the material to be taught and to design a plan for the teaching.

13. **Those planning adult classes should consider whether they need a special class for those who come, but are not yet members of the church or for recent converts.** These people likely need studies that are more foundational than the typical adult class is using. They also may need a different style of teaching that is more open and less structured than other adult classes. Eventually these people will need to find their way into the regular classes, so they may have fellowship with those with whom they have much in common. Some congregations have used their "seekers" class as a major tool to bring in people who are not members of the church. They advertise it, suggest that only members who bring a non-member may attend it, and build it into their local evangelism program.

14. **It is extremely important to have an effective Vacation Bible School.** Such events are an important cog in the wheel of educational experiences. Those who are children in the church can learn much from this concentrated experience, and they can learn a little about evangelism as they are encouraged to bring a friend. And families should seek to bring the children of neighbors. The tendency today is to shorten VBS, but the teachers need to have enough time with the students to make a strong impression and to teach some valuable lessons. One congregation has stations for its VBS, and the children

move from station to station. That means that the teacher teaches the same lesson several times and consequently has less preparation to do. One of the stations on their list is an application station where the teacher knows what they have been studying and asks, "So what?"

Even though VBS is an important tool for the typical congregation, it can be extra special for a small church. If you are from a church that does not have enough teachers to carry out a good VBS, ask some larger congregation not too far away to help you. Most would be glad to do it. Maybe you could study the same VBS lessons as they did. Perhaps some of their teachers could help with your program using the same material. In a smaller town the VBS can be well-advertised, and members can be enlisted to work hard at bringing those who are not members. This can make the VBS one of the best outreach times of your year. Of course, all congregations need to find out who the VBS visitors are, get information from them for further contact, and have a systematic plan for reaching out to them after VBS is over to encourage them to be regular attenders. A congregation without a strong follow-up program for VBS is missing a great opportunity to reach people who will listen.

15. **The educational director or chairman of the education committee should be sure that there are training sessions for teachers.** The simplest way to do this is to have a more experienced teacher in your congregation meet with a group of teachers prior to the beginning of a quarter to review with them the content of the materials and some specific methods they might use. Or you might bring in someone from outside the congregation to do this. A church can have a seminar for its teachers using two or three well-qualified people to direct the sessions. And sometimes there are churches or Christian schools that conduct seminars to help teachers learn more about teaching. Another good way to develop teachers is to have a less experienced teacher assist a more experienced teacher for a quarter or longer. One who is charged with overseeing the educational program in a church of any size should have the training of those who can become effective teachers in the program on his list of regular things to do.

The person in charge of the educational program should not neglect opportunities to learn from others. He might visit another church to get good ideas or might attend seminars on teaching.

16. **Those in charge of the education program should be creative in finding good teachers.** They can ask for volunteers, but sometimes, they need to note people who are not teaching, but who are or who could become good teachers. They should approach such people and ask them to teach or prepare to teach. There are those who would be willing if asked, but who are not inclined to volunteer. These new teachers can be assigned to a shorter time span to "test the waters" to see how they are doing before they are assigned to teach for a full term.

17. **Those in charge of Bible School should be sure that there are strong efforts to increase attendance.**

    a. Have a plan to follow up on every local visitor to encourage that person to become a regular attender. If the visitor attended a class, someone in that class may be charged with this responsibility or there may be a group of people who will volunteer to do this follow-up, but every Bible School program should have a plan in operation to be sure visitors are contacted. If the person also attended a church service, a different person could also make contact to give information and encouragement about continuing to attend. This may be by letter, by a call, or by a visit. Those who visit from the local community are certainly among the best prospects for long-term additions to the class and, ultimately, perhaps for conversion.

    b. There should be a plan to follow up with every visitor to VBS through a visit to encourage the person to become a regular attender. If that visitor was a child whose parents do not attend, make sure the visit includes information about classes for the adults in the family as well as the child.

    c. Each quarter when new classes are starting, an effort should be made to get members of the congregation not attending either Sunday morning or Wednesday night classes to start. These efforts can be encouraged on the basis of growing in Bible knowledge and on improving fellowship with other Christians. On Wednesday nights, for example, each quarter should have a class that holds special appeal for those not attending regularly. That may be a study of Revelation and Last Days. It may be a study of prophecies about Jesus or on parenting or financial peace. Just find some good topic which will rely on Bible teaching that meets the interests and/or needs of those not attending. Then push through the bulletin, public announcements, mailings, encouragement from elders, and other methods exactly what the benefits will be for those attending the class. An article and/or advertisement in the local paper can also be helpful, and members can be given brochures about the class they can use to encourage attendance from outsiders as well as from members. An elder may make a public statement about the benefits of attending and other ways should be developed to encourage those attending church to start attending classes.

d. Occasionally, you might want to bring in a special teacher for a class on Wednesday nights or for a special seminar to kick off a quarter.

e. Publish class descriptions using a meaningful course title and description. Find many ways to make this information available—bulletin, posters in the lobby, handouts.

f. Be creative, but always keep in mind the need to get as many as possible to attend classes.

18. **Most of us do not do enough to express appreciation to those who teach in the educational programs of the church.** Unfortunately, many have taught for years who have never had a word of appreciation from the elders or even from the educational director. One never gets too old to appreciate being appreciated. Some churches have periodic dinners for their teachers and make it a special occasion. Others send cards or provide gift cards to express appreciation or find other ways to say "thanks." One who teaches a quarter of classes may well spend two or three hours a week in preparation for a total of 40-50 hours. That is a lot of time and effort, and some teach year round. So those directing the education program need to find creative ways to thank their teachers on a regular basis.

The educational program in any church is one of its most important functions. Through this program, the members can achieve the objectives listed above, grow spiritually, strengthen their relationships with other members, and reach out to the lost. With such potential good to be done, the Bible School Program should be the best it can be.

CHAPTER 6

THE MISSIONS PROGRAM

Can be its Best

That Christ intended His followers to be mission-minded is clear from His final words to the apostles. As mentioned in the previous chapter, Matthew's account says to go, make disciples, baptize, and teach (Matthew 28:19). According to Mark's account we are to "Go into all the world and preach the gospel to every creature. He that believes and is baptized shall be saved" (Mark 16:15-16).

Our going may be by sending a missionary who preaches and teaches or through a missionary who teaches others to teach. In our day, this work may be by printed material, correspondence courses, a website, email, or through social media. And, as in the first century, teaching can certainly be done one-on-one. By any means possible and anywhere possible, then, we are to go, make disciples, baptize, and teach people to follow "the apostles' teaching" for the rest of their lives. Eventually, then, we can judge the success of mission work by its success in spreading the word, baptizing, and follow-up teaching to strengthen those saved.

Here is a checklist of ideas to help an eldership or missions committee or missionaries in thinking about how best to carry the gospel to the whole world in our day. (The information below applies to both men and women who serve in various mission capacities but the wording used will typically be masculine.)

1. **Choose the missionary carefully.** Congregations usually have many opportunities to find people to support.

HOW THE MISSIONS PROGRAMS *Can be its Best*

a. Try to produce missionaries from among your own members. It is great when a church can bring up missionaries from its own young people. Teach your youth about mission work, and take them on mission trips.

b. Investigate carefully anyone who asks for support whom you may become interested in helping. Check their background fully. What training have they had? What previous experience? Do their references show they have done well in their education and in any previous work? Did they get their training at a school you know about and are comfortable with? In their interview, do they appear to be the type of person with whom you can work? Do they have good answers to your questions? Are they experienced or is this their first venture? Do they have a plan to keep you well-informed? Be sure to have a doctrinal questionnaire that will ask them to provide their position in writing on key issues. You don't want to help support someone who will establish congregations that do not share your view of the fundamentals.

Some of the aforementioned questions would need to be altered if you are thinking of working with a native of the country where they will be doing their work. Before you make such a connection, it would be good to provide the means for that person to visit your church so you can know the person and the person can know you. Supporting people in their native country has the advantage of one who already knows the language and culture of that country. It can, however, have the disadvantage of making the church where he or she works to become dependent on the sending church and not, therefore, growing in accepting its own responsibilities. Maybe a plan can be devised that allows you to support fully a native preacher, for example, for two years at a church. By then the goal could be for that church to take on a fourth of his support, and then year by year to grow in that support until they are fully supporting him. Maybe during that time he cannot only be growing that church in its responsibilities, but can be training someone local to become the fully supported preacher there. Then he can move on to start another congregation with your help.

2. **Choose the location carefully.** Churches have many opportunities to do mission work and should use the following criteria in determining just where they want to spend their resources for missions.

    a. Do you choose the location because of your study of where you believe your money can be best spent to do the Lord's work or do you choose the location because someone comes to you already knowing where he or she wants to go? There is not necessarily a right or wrong answer to this question, but you should give consideration to it before deciding on a location.

    b. What results do you expect? It is not wise to judge a location based purely on how many baptisms the person can produce each year but, on the other hand, you don't want to spend large sums of money in a place so unreceptive that no progress is being made. One church, for example, spent thousands of dollars to support a two-family team in a location where a small church had already been begun. After two years, one of the families returned home because of differences with the other. After another three or four years, the church decided that so little progress was being made that they made the tough decision to spend no more there and chose to spend their money elsewhere.

    c. Right now, countries in Africa and the nation of India appear to be the most responsive places to spread the Word. Some places in Europe are doing better than they were for a while because the churches there are reaching refugees who are more responsive than the natives there. Some works in Central and South America are progressing well, usually where there is some combination of serving the local community while sharing the gospel. And in rural America, some churches are dying and might be strengthened if the right person were sent to work with them. There are many factors to weigh when deciding on a location to support.

3. **Determine the type of work you want to support.** There are many ways to spread the Word. You can support a preacher at a congregation or a preacher who travels among congregations. You can support a nurse or a doctor, who will work in a medical clinic that helps people needing medical care and who, in the process, reaches them for Christ. You can

support one who teaches, preaches, and/or writes material. You can support a Bible school, an orphanage, a hospital, or a preacher training school. Any of these might be good, and they contribute to the spread of the gospel in different ways.

4. **Try to focus your mission efforts.** Some congregation give a small amount to several different works, but it is better, in most cases, to narrow your approach. The more connected the congregation feels with the missionaries you support, the more likely they are to give more generously to help them. So if, when you are selling your budget to the congregation they are challenged to give more to help a missionary they know well, you will probably raise more money for the work. Some congregations even use Skype software or some similar method to allow the missionary on the field to give a report to the congregation about his work during a Sunday morning service leading up to the start of the new budget year. And when the missionary comes back to the country for his bi-annual break, those leading in the mission effort have him bring a lesson to the church.

5. **Consider whether the mission work you are sponsoring will reach more people if it has an element of serving people with health services, education opportunities, caring for orphans and widows, providing a water well, or some other type of assistance.** Helping people is, of course, a command of Christ (Matthew 25:31-46; Galatians 6:10). So we serve others to "do good for them," but we also do it as a way of letting our light shine to attract them to want to know more about Jesus. Sometimes people become so absorbed by the helping aspects that they do not give enough attention to the teaching aspects, so a good balance must be followed.

6. **Will the use of correspondence courses from World Bible School or some other similar source enhance the work of your missionary?** Often people who would not be willing to come hear a preacher are willing to read and even to complete the first lesson in one of these courses. Thus, the correspondence course can become a good entering wedge. Members of your congregation can grade the lessons sent from the country where your missionary works and write to prospects whom he can contact when they are ready. This is a good way to connect your

members and your missionary. You can find World Bible School online.
7. **There are many ways you can help the missionary you have chosen to support.** His salary should be adequate for his living expenses and to provide the opportunity for saving some for retirement. He also should have, in addition to his salary, a work fund that allows him to travel as needed for his work, to buy supplies, to help the congregation with special needs. Be sure to keep up with the exchange rate. You may think you have given a raise, but it may be absorbed by changes in what US dollars purchase in another country.

    The support, however, should go far beyond the monetary. In the years he or she does not come back home, someone from the congregation, an elder or mission leader should go to see the missionary. This both encourages the person and allows the congregation to know more about the work. Someone in the congregation should be designated as the special contact for each missionary you support, and that person should make phone calls, correspond with email, or use Skype software or some similar tool. Others in the congregation should write notes of appreciation. Those who have not experienced leaving one's home country to live elsewhere for many years do not understand how much it means to have regular and encouraging contact.

8. **There should be regular and frequent informational contact between the missionary and his supporting church.** The missionary, for example, should make regular reports to his supporting congregation. These may be monthly, bi-monthly, or quarterly, depending on the nature of the work. The reports should include information about what the missionary has been doing, what results he or she has been having, and something about the missionary's personal and family life. Many missionaries, as they report, try to acquaint members of their supporting church with the individuals with whom they are studying, so all can pray for them and rejoice when they come to Christ. The supporting church should use the information in these reports to help their members feel connected with the missionary and, thus, to want to provide support for his work.

    Elders, mission committees, and even the whole congregation will benefit from some basic introduction to intercultural communication. A foreign culture is often drastically different from the culture of the sponsoring congregation. Understanding the differences will make healthy communication more likely between the sponsoring church and those on the field.

Another important type of contact with missionaries is for the supporting church to send representatives to see first-hand the work that person and his family are doing. Even if this means spending a considerable amount on travel expenses, such contact is vitally important. For one thing, it gives the missionary a sense of the importance the congregation places on his work. Another important result is the stronger connection such visits give the congregation with the work. If, over the years, three or four different people have made these visits, and if they have been well-impressed with the work, they will become strong advocates on behalf of the work. If, for example, the missionary and his family are given a bi-annual trip back home, the visits to see his work could be on the alternate years.

9. **The missions committee, or whoever is overseeing the work of the missionary, should make an annual evaluation of his work.** Contributing to this evaluation can be the bi-annual visit by someone in the congregation and the bi-annual visit home in alternate years. Each year the missionary should submit goals he hopes to reach during the coming year, and he should follow up at the end of that year with a report of the progress made toward the goals. The "go, disciple, baptize, and teach" model should lie in the background of evaluating the work. Not only are the numbers being baptized important, but how well are those baptized being taught the Word and learning to do their part in the work of the church. Knowing that this evaluation will be made each year gives the missionary a target to reach and gives the committee a basis for signaling their approval or concerns. This evaluation should include a review of the adequacy of the salary in light of changes in currency rates and family circumstances. The atmosphere of this review, of course, should be more a review of achievements than an occasion of criticism, but if sufficient progress is not being made, the recommendation for a change may need to come.

10. **When the missionary decides to move back to his or her home country, the congregation should be ready to help.** This is a pretty traumatic experience. The missionary and family have been immersed in a different culture for several years. The children in the family may never have lived in the United States. The adjustment to all of this is often difficult. This being the case, the supporting church should provide a few months of opportunity for the returning family to have support while they get situated in another job and for getting adjusted to their new circumstances.

    Each year, there is a conference at Oklahoma Christian University to help these returning missionaries and their children to help make the adjustment. The children in these cases, are called "third-culture kids" because they have grown up in one culture and are now having to adjust to another culture, and such a combination means they are actually living in a third culture. This conference, typically held in July, has been beneficial to a large number of families. Often they have been having trouble with the adjustment and didn't understand why. This conference helps them to know that what is happening is not unusual, but is instead, typical. To find out about the conference, contact *kent.hartman@oc.edu* or the College of Biblical Studies at OC.

So, the Lord wants every congregation to have a strong mission program built around "go, disciple, baptize, and teach." Find ways to make your program fit this model.

CHAPTER 7

 THE LOCAL OUTREACH PROGRAM

Can be its Best

If congregations were evaluated on the efforts they make to carry out what God wants a local church to do, the lowest marks in most congregations would go to their local outreach programs. We tend to do foreign missions, education, benevolence, and care of the building better than we do local outreach. Yet sharing the gospel message locally is the most important thing we can do. It should be our top priority.

The story in Acts about the growth of the church tells of people who were scattered by persecution and when they got to their next location, they still told people about Jesus (Acts 8:1). In the next centuries, when there was heavy persecution of Christians and letting people know about your faith in Jesus might mean imprisonment or death, Christianity still grew rapidly because church members still told the story. People were also impressed by the way Christians lived, the way they served others, and the way they died in the arenas, going to death because of Jesus, while singing praises to Him. These early Christians should be an inspiration to us to share our faith in a country where there is little likelihood of any bad outcome.

In our day, a general observation is that Christians are afraid to talk to people about Jesus and the church because they think something undesirable will come as a result. It is never altogether clear what that bad thing is. Though in some locations the danger is real, in the U.S., imprisonment or physical harm is highly unlikely. Rarely would anything

HOW THE LOCAL OUTREACH PROGRAM *Can be its Best*

take place like a loss of a job or isolation from other employees. It isn't even likely that a next-door neighbor is going to become mean because a Christian asks her to church. A kind invitation is unlikely to break a relationship. But still many are afraid. It is true that our culture is growing less religious, but it is not true that we are taking much risk to share our faith with others. Our churches do not plan carefully for local outreach and, in many churches, there are not even events anymore designed to bring non-members to the church building.

Yet, we all know that the great commission calls on us to spread the message (Matthew 28:18-20). The command is to "go, therefore, and make disciples." That directive isn't just for missionaries or paid staff to go and make disciples. Jesus even says that when we are carrying out the command to go, make disciples, baptize people, and teach them more, "I will be with you always." And that "you" includes all of us.

Some churches have outstanding programs of local outreach and baptize many during a year. Most churches, however, have little or no plan for reaching out in the local community and so convert few and are in a declining mode.

This chapter offers a host of ideas about what churches can do to improve their local outreach. There are many possible things to do that are not expensive and are not difficult. This chapter will list a large number of actions both at the congregational level and at the individual level. So, at this point, do two things: Recognize this is an area that needs improvement, and commit yourself to finding out from this chapter some specific actions you and your congregation will take.

1. **Create a ministry or committee for local evangelism.** Many congregations have an education committee, a building committee, a missions committee, and a worship committee. Most, however, have no committee or ministry for local outreach. If a congregation wants to make important and continuing steps in this area, they must have a permanent group of dedicated people who are committed to meeting frequently, at least once or twice a month, to discuss things to implement for the congregation to do and for individual members to do. They must be taking a long-term view by setting some goals and evaluating what is happening about achieving those goals. They will

serve under the elders and will make regular reports and suggestions to the elders, but they should be empowered to carry out many useful actions on their own.

The committee should be made up of men and women who have a strong commitment to planning things for others to do and to participating in doing these things themselves. One small congregation that was slipping in membership had a group who asked the elders if they could meet weekly to discuss ways to reach local people with the gospel. The elders agreed and within about two years, the church had grown by 50 percent.

The ministry group for a congregation should review things mentioned below and should also obtain a copy of the book *Evangelizing Your Community* from 21st Century Christian by calling 1-800-251-2477. This book is filled with specific suggestions, only some of which are in this chapter.

Below is a list of things to which this evangelism ministry and individual Christians should give particular attention.

1. **The local outreach committee should:**
   a. See that every visitor is greeted at the door and shown where to attend class and worship, and is greeted again as they leave.
   b. Obtain sufficient information to do follow up by a phone call, a visit, and a letter for every visitor. Those local people who visit a service are excellent prospects for more contact. One church buys coffee mugs with the name of the church printed on it, puts a few printed items of information about the church in the mug, and has someone to deliver it to the house of the Sunday visitor by Monday. If they are home, the visitor warmly thanks them for coming and gives them the mug. If they are not home, the visitor leaves the mug at the front door, after all, a dog will not bother a cup. And who will throw away a coffee mug? So here is a long-term reminder. One man who "worked the lobby" met the visitors, called and wrote them the next week, invited them to lunch when they came the second time, then asked to have a Bible study with them. He sometimes baptized 20 people a year by greeting them warmly as they came in the building and by doing the follow-up.

HOW THE LOCAL OUTREACH PROGRAM *Can be its Best*

    c. Make a list of people who attend your services regularly, but have never been baptized. Maybe the wife or husband of a member or someone who has grown up in the church but is now in their 20s or 30s and has not been baptized. The committee should develop the best strategy for approaching each one on the list, perhaps with the help of a relative. Maybe someone starts developing a special friendship with the person or maybe the person is asked to be part of a service project the church is doing. The committee thinks about ways to strengthen the ties and then, when the time is right, makes the move to visit with the person about becoming a Christian. One church had a visiting preacher to play golf with one such attender so he could visit with him as they were in the golf cart. He was soon baptized.

    d. Make a list of those who have dropped away from the church over the last 10 years. Consider why they fell away and develop a strategy for who should contact them and how. Bringing such people back must be a key effort of the congregation. One smaller church made a list of 50 who had left, planned a special Sunday service for such people to return, and used mail and visits to invite them. Twenty-five of these people attended the special day, and some of them continued to attend. Jesus spoke of the good shepherd who made great effort to bring back a lost sheep; it's a message we should take most seriously. To let people slip away unnoticed is certainly not what Christ wants to happen. So we should be alert for those beginning to miss services and to seek to draw them back. Showing an interest in them, re-connecting them with friends, and finding a church job for them to do can all be part of a plan to rescue them. Maybe they left over some issue that needs to be resolved. Each case, of course, is different, but a careful plan should be laid and carried out along with prayer.

    e. Plan a training program to teach all members of the church—high school and older—how to explain the gospel message in a simple, but compelling, way. (See the book on *Evangelizing Your Community* for a good method to use.)

f. Along with the "how to explain the message," also teach everyone from children through adults the need to use conversational evangelism and friendship evangelism to reach people. Help them to practice these approaches in role-playing in Wednesday night classes and then to report on what they did during the week at the next class meeting.

g. Plan events that will draw people to church—a seminar on parenting, on marriage, on financial peace, or a weekend series on the Book of Revelation. Get the whole church involved in advertising these events to get the largest number possible of non-members to attend. Put an ad in the local paper, and inquire whether the paper might also print a story about the event. Then have a plan for follow up to encourage visitors who attend to have a Bible study and/or attend church services.

h. Have a Friend's Day at least once a year and get members to submit names of friends they will contact so the church can mail them an invitation. This, along with the friends' personal invitations can bring a good number of non–members to attend. And plan how to follow-up with those who come so they will continue to attend. One church worked their Friend's Day so well that after a few years they had to have two services on Sunday mornings to accommodate all the friends who came. They brought a speaker with impressive credentials from out-of-town as the speaker, and members worked hard to bring friends. This event became one of the major events of the year in this smaller town.

i. Develop a connection with a local high school or elementary school. Members can help tutor or chaperone events when the students go on trips. The church can provide backpacks filled with good school supplies for children who need them. And the church can help provide teachers with supplies they need. This will make a good impression on many and, thus, can lay the foundation for other types of contact.

j. Plan to involve church members in ways to gain goodwill in the community. Clean up a local park, have members coach little league teams, clean up a portion of a highway, regularly have a high school sports team to the building for a meal after a game, help with FFA or similar groups, establish an after-school program for children whose parents don't come home from work until 5 p.m. The church needs a good name in town, so the committee should think of the best ways to build that relationship in their particular community.

k. Have a Vacation Bible School to teach your children, but also to make good contacts with outside families. Get members to bring the children of friends. Then, after the VBS, be sure to follow up with invitations and visits to those non-member families who sent children to keep them coming. If the congregation is too small to have a VBS on its own, invite some other church to provide some teachers and others to help. These guests could even help with door-to-door visits about VBS the week before it starts. This activity will be good for both churches.

l. Train members to teach home Bible studies and one-on-one studies and help them find ways to get started doing these studies. The church leaders and members of the committee should lead the way in doing such studies.

2. **The church needs a good benevolent program.** Depending on local circumstances, the church should develop a plan to help those who are in need. This plan may include such things as a meal program, clothing, providing a back-to-school backpack, inner-city assistance, disaster relief, or other ways that fit the local needs. The Bible certainly teaches us to care for those in need, and each congregation should be known for doing this. Be sure to follow up with those helped to take advantage of the opportunity to teach them about the Bible after you have helped them. One church I know about makes the follow up on the benevolence program its primary effort in reaching the lost.

3. **The preacher should occasionally preach sermons about how to become a Christian both to inform and encourage those attending who have not been baptized and to teach the congregation about the conversion process.** If a topic is never the subject of sermons, the congregation will think it is not important. The preacher should also deliver sermons about how members should be active in reaching

out to others. He must be a key player in local evangelism, not only in speaking about it, but also in having Bible studies himself with those who are not Christians.

4. **Through the pulpit and classes for all ages, the church should emphasize the importance of Christian living as a means of evangelism.** Jesus said in Matthew 5:16 that we are to be a light to the world, and that when people see our good works, they will glorify God. Teach the congregation how to be a light at school, on the job, in the neighborhood, in sports, in organizations, on the golf course, and even in driving your car. An elderly couple who were Christians were spending a little time at the beach. After being there three days going to the same chairs and umbrella, a woman came and asked how long they had been married. The number of years was more than 60, and the woman told them that she had been most impressed with the way they treated each other. As the conversation continued, the Christian man found that the inquiring woman lived where he once had lived and they talked about that a bit. Then he told where they went to church while there and asked the woman where they went. The woman said she attended a church, but had not approved of some of the changes her church had recently made and was looking for a new one. Of course the man told her about the church, and the woman said she would check it out. "Let your light shine."

   Having gained good will through Christian living, the door is open to invite people to a special event such as a Friend's Day or a VBS or lessons on special topics. Christian living paves the way for more direct evangelism.

5. **Each member should learn to practice conversational evangelism.** The New Testament is filled with examples of people informally talking with others about spiritual matters. Consider Jesus with the woman at the well (John 4), Jesus with the sinful woman (John 8), Philip and the Ethiopian (Acts 8), Paul in the marketplace (Acts 17), Paul speaking with Agrippa (Acts 26), Paul in the house in Rome (Acts 28), and many more. We should, as appropriate, mention to non-Christians things like a service Christians are giving others, an

activity of the youth, an upcoming seminar, a high school student at church who has done something of interest, a useful point a preacher made in a sermon, a verse of Scripture we have read, or the recent funeral of a Christian. We should learn to be skillful in finding ways to bring up something with a spiritual twist in our conversations. These comments can, in time, lead us to bring up more significant matters and lay the groundwork for asking someone to study the Bible with us or to attend church services. The preacher should speak about Bible cases of conversational evangelism and show people how to do that type of outreach today. Wednesday night classes can encourage people to do conversational evangelism and give them an opportunity to practice doing it and to report to the class on how they have actually done this the previous week.

6. **The next step after conversational evangelism is friendship evangelism.** Those who study conversions in all churches say that more are reached through friend connections than any other. So, to make a congregation evangelistic, members must be trained for and encouraged in friendship evangelism. The greatest barrier to speaking with friends about spiritual matters seems to be fear of offending. Again, those who study these matters say that it is highly unlikely that a friend will be offended by a non-threatening comment or invitation. Of course if we are in "attack mode," something unfortunate might happen, but an appropriate invitation to a service, to a Friends Day, to a church service on Resurrection Sunday or Christmas, or to a special seminar is certainly not going to offend. And people seem to respond better to an invitation to a special event than to just a regular Sunday service. When we have built a good foundation by doing things together, an occasional comment about good things happening at church or invitation for a Bible study will be the thing to do. A congregation should teach members regularly about the need to work with friends and even should provide for some good practice sessions for role-playing maybe on a Wednesday night.

7. **An important need in local evangelism is follow-up with those who are converted.** A plan should be in place to connect one or more members with the person who is baptized. Several should send notes

of congratulations. Some should be prepared to invite them into their home. A special class for those recently converted can help them learn more about being a good follower of Christ and about getting involved in the work of the church. One of the most important ways to secure a new member is to put them quickly to work in some type of service: benevolence, helping with a children's class, going to see visitors who have attended, work around the building, helping in benevolence, or helping with a home Bible study.

8. **An effective way to promote local evangelism is to tell the stories of those who are being converted.** Use a video for the church to see or have the preacher or someone else in the worship service to tell the story of a recent convert who came to Christ. Tell how they were first contacted, who was involved in teaching the person, and who helped him/her to make a decision to be baptized. Sharing these stories, either at the time of their baptism or at some other time soon after, will inspire others to share the gospel. Stories of how a person came to faith can be moving.

9. **Have an evangelism workshop or seminar at your congregation to encourage not only your members but the members of other congregations in your area to be more active in local outreach.** Local preachers can conduct the sessions, or those planning the event may want to bring in someone from outside to speak.

10. **Those planning the classes for Sunday morning and for Wednesday night should occasionally work into the curriculum some sessions to teach about how the early church did local outreach and the different ways in which members can be involved.** These sessions should cover questions that a prospect may ask such as, "Why is there evil and suffering in the world?" or "Why are there so many different churches?" The classes could even include some role-playing that puts a member in a situation in which he/she can practice what they could say in various situations to help someone attend a service or be willing to have a Bible study.

11. **Another way to do local outreach is through an international program.** Most places have those who have come from other countries. Many

of these do not know English well and are interested in finding a place to learn it. Many churches take advantage of this opportunity by offering a program called "Let's Start Talking," which uses the Book of Luke to teach English. After all, those wanting to read and speak must have something in English to use. By making people and materials available for the study of English, internationals can be attracted, and as they use the Bible to read and discuss, they often become interested in knowing more about it. The church can provide worship services, Bible study groups, and opportunities for fellowship for these individuals.

12. **Many churches use jail and prison ministries as a means of local outreach.** In some prisons they are able to conduct Bible study classes and in local jails, they are often allowed to circulate correspondence courses. They get the first lesson in the hands of a person in jail and give that person an extra copy of the first lesson, which he/she can share with others. By this means, they keep the studies going. When the person has completed several lessons, it is time for someone from the church to teach the person directly by whatever means the jail leaders will make available. By using a portable baptistery, the church can occasionally go into the jail to baptize those who have studied to that point. Of course, continuing contact after that is necessary. To get information about correspondence materials to use for jail/prison work, contact the prison ministry at the Memorial Road Church of Christ in Oklahoma City, Oklahoma. You can reach them by phone at 405.478.1168.

13. **As with everything in our congregational and personal lives, there should be prayer.** Public prayers should mention evangelism and a private prayer group could be praying for specific ones who are trying to be reached and for those members who are working with them. A private prayer group could offer petitions for Bible studies, for those recently converted, and for young people who are so important in the future of the church. As with all elements of God's work, we need to be praying for our work in local outreach.

A congregation should be mobilized for local outreach with a good ministry or committee working regularly to see that the basic things in local outreach are being done and that members are being trained to do their part. Plans should be made regularly to gain a good name in the community. And the church should use sermons and classes to emphasize how members can be active in outreach through Christian living and through their contacts. Prayers should be offered, and the leaders of the church should be showing the way.

THE BENEVOLENCE PROGRAM

Can be its Best

One of Jesus' strongest teachings is that we should visit the sick, feed the hungry, and give a drink of water to the thirsty. In fact, in Matthew 25 He mentions such activities as the only matters on which the final judgment will be based. We learn from other passages, of course, that more factors will be involved in that judgment, but surely this is Jesus' way of emphasizing how important benevolent activities are. According to Acts 2:45, soon after the church began, the believers were following what Jesus said to do because those who had possessions were selling them to care for members who were in need. In Acts 6:1-3 we learn that the apostles made sure that Grecian widows were having their needs met. Paul wrote to the Corinthians about the importance of the funds he was collecting among the Gentile churches to take to Jerusalem to help Jewish Christians who were in need. And in Galatians 6:10, Paul encourages caring for the needy by telling the church to "be good to everyone, especially those of the household of faith." So we cannot be the church of Jesus Christ and not be caring for those in need, both through the church and individually.

In this chapter, we will think first about some general principles to guide us in our benevolent work and then list different opportunities for Christians to show their generous spirit. Our purpose in this chapter is to provide a wide range of possibilities for benevolent work, which elders, those leading in a congregation's benevolent work, or even an individual can review to see if they might find something they could add to what

HOW THE BENEVOLENCE PROGRAM *Can be its Best*

they are currently doing. We will also provide some suggestions so those individuals who do benevolent work might make improvements.

General Principles for Doing Benevolence Work

1. When Jesus taught the Parable of the Good Samaritan, He taught that we should love everyone and do good for others whether there are any side benefits for us or not. Helping people is just the right thing to do. Even if we do not have the opportunity to tell people we are from the church, and even if they don't even know who helped them, we should rise to help people in need, not "passing by on the other side."

2. Galatians 6:10 says for us to "do good unto all, especially those of the household of faith." Even though we are to do good for everyone, we should make a special effort to care for members of the church. Sometimes churches have special programs to help the poor outside the church, but have no systematic way of helping their fellow Christians. Christians in need are often reluctant to ask for help because the church has not made known that it wants to help them.

    The early church in Jerusalem had an excellent program for helping the needy among them. People even sold houses and land and took the money to the apostles who could distribute it as needed. Their care for one another was noted by outsiders because "they were held in favor by all the people" (Acts 2:47). I once heard of a Christian man who was badly injured in a car accident and had to move about in a wheelchair. His friends from the church with carpentry skills went to his house to widen the doors, make changes in the bathroom, and put a ramp up to the front door. The neighbors asked the man's wife who these people were because they didn't come in panel trucks with the name of their company on the side. She told them they were friends from the church. Soon, a Bible study with the neighbors began, and they were baptized—beginning with Christians helping Christians in need.

3. First Corinthians 10:31 says that "whatever you do, do it all for the glory of God" (NIV). When people know we are Christians and they see us helping the poor, caring for a member in need, or feeding people on Thanksgiving Day, they will recognize that we are doing what Christian

people should do, and this will bring God the glory. Though we will not always have a way to let people know we are connected with Christ, when we can, we should. For instance, I know of a family that was converted and has been faithful because when their house burned, it was Christian neighbors who were the first to come to help.

4. James 1:27 says that pure religion is to "look after widows and orphans in their distress." As individuals and as the church, then, we should have plans to help widows and orphans. First Timothy 5:2-16 gives some additional instructions about this topic saying that the church should especially concern itself with caring for older widows who have no way of caring for themselves and who have served others well both in their homes and in caring for others. Paul makes the point that a woman's relatives should care for her if they can, so the church will not be burdened, but if she has no such provisions, then the church should help her.

From these passages we learn several principles. The church should spend its money wisely by caring for those who have no one else to help them. Particularly, the church should be helping those who have shown themselves worthy as Christians. Some judgment should, then, be exercised in deciding how to spend money in helping others. Are those asking for help deserving of that help? Could family members help them? Could they be supporting themselves? An effort should be made to apply these principles even though in some cases there is no way to know for sure. Some have said it is better to help someone who may not be deserving than to turn away someone who is deserving. As with many passages of Scripture, we use it as a guide and make the wisest application we can.

5. In Acts 6, the apostles authorized a program to help Grecian widows who were being neglected in the daily distribution of food. They determined that seven men were needed for this particular work, and they asked the congregation to come up with the names of those whom they could appoint. This passage makes it clear that churches should have an efficient, well-led, and well-organized program for helping those it needs to serve.

HOW THE BENEVOLENCE PROGRAM *Can be its Best*

Types of Benevolent Work That Congregations Should Consider Doing

1. **Preaching and classes should encourage members and even children to be helpful to those around them.** Although several types of work for the congregation are listed below that require leaders, every congregation should encourage its members to be helpful to the needy around them. One member, who lives in an area where it occasionally snows in the winter, keeps a tractor with a blade in the front at his home. He uses it to get out early to clear snow off the streets in the neighborhood, so those living there can reach the streets that the local government has cleared. Another Christian man gets up early and walks around his neighborhood after the papers have been thrown and takes them to the front door of each home. This makes him a favorite neighbor and opens opportunities to visit with people about church.

    Others care for neighbors who are ill, mow the lawns of those away on vacation, buy groceries for an elderly neighbor who has trouble getting around, and drive older widows to doctor's appointments. A high school student can tutor a friend who has missed classes due to illness, in an effort to help her catch up on school work. I know Christian men who coach a little league team, so they can have contact with families who have children whom they can invite to church. People at work can help fellow employees who have had to miss work to be with a sick child or parent. A farmer can plow the sick neighbor's field or bale his hay. We can apply this principle to our driving so that we let someone else go first at the corner, let someone into the line who is coming out of an adjoining road, or even help someone who is stalled along the side of the road although we need to use care about this one.

    Jesus taught us to "love our neighbors." Even though the word *neighbor* includes everyone all over the world whom we can help, it certainly includes those next door or at the next desk with whom we have contact. We want to be helpful to those needing care, but often such contact can also lead us to opportunities of inviting people to church or having a Bible study.

    Preachers should have sermons not only to encourage members to love their neighbors, but also to tell them how. Bible classes on

Sunday morning and on Wednesday night can teach on the subject and let members share about things they have done to encourage others to do the same. Always include not only a study of the passages of Scripture, but also make sure to provide specific applications of how to do the helpful services.

2. **A congregation should have a room in which they keep canned goods and other non-perishable food as well as clothing donated by members so they can have such items on hand to help people as needed.** I know a congregation that designates a Sunday about twice a year to asking members to bring bags of unperishable food they have purchased at the grocery store and place them on the platform at the front of the building as they arrive. Many members involve their children in the purchase of this food and in bringing it to the front as they enter the building. As the platform begins to show lots of bags of food, and as elders or the preacher thank those who have participated, members feel satisfaction from what they have done, and others are encouraged to participate in the next food drive. Members should occasionally be encouraged to bring usable clothing and shoes to put in the room. And someone should be designated to keep the clothing and food in good order so those coming for help can work with someone from the church to find what they need.

3. **Designate specific individuals to work with those who come to the building asking for help.** Sometimes these are local people who have fallen on bad times, and sometimes they are travelers who have had a problem that has left them stranded. The congregation should have a fund set aside to help such people, and the designated people can use this fund as they deem necessary. This is not an easy job, yet it can be satisfying to know that you have helped someone in need. Since there are sometimes people who will make up a story about their needs and use this as a way of collecting money, it is wise to provide the care by giving them food and clothing rather than money. You might even have $15 or $20 gift cards to an inexpensive local restaurant where they can get a meal or gift cards for a local service station. If the person coming is local, then any help provided should also come with an invitation to come to church or with the first lesson of a correspondence program.

THE BENEVOLENCE PROGRAM *Can be its Best*

4. **The congregation should also designate someone to help its own members who need help, and the congregation should know that such help is available.** This assistance may include a meeting with someone trained in helping people with their budgeting, so the person can have a well-designed plan to work out of the hole in which he finds himself. Some may need food or clothing from the storeroom or may need some monetary help to pay bills because of a job loss. There are occasions when a health problem may cost a large sum, and the congregation or a Bible class will want to take a special contribution to help. If such is the case, it should be approved by the elders as a special work of the church so that contributions can be given through the church and, thus, used as a tax deduction. When congregations help their own members, they are building up goodwill within their own ranks and sending the message that they love each other as Christ has taught us to do. The congregation can keep the membership aware that because of the love members have for one another, help is available when it is needed. Often outsiders hear of such assistance and are impressed with the church for doing that.

5. **The congregation may have various organized efforts in benevolence and may find different ways for the congregation to participate.**
    a. Orphan homes. Many congregations work with orphan homes in their area particularly orphan homes connected with the church, to assist with funding in various ways. Some put the homes in their budget and send a regular amount to them each year. Others send an envelope around in adult Bible classes to collect funds for orphan homes beyond the regular budget. A designated person picks up the envelopes and sends the money to the homes. Some congregations work with the homes to collect food and/or clothing, and the home sends a truck to pick it up. Still others send a crew to the home to help with landscaping, painting, or similar work. Finally, some churches regularly send members to a home to work with the children by showing interest in them by taking them out to eat, playing games, or doing other things the home believes helpful. The friendships established sometimes result in long-term connections, which allows children to visit the people with whom

they have made this contact. Every congregation should have some relationship with Christian children's homes who are seeking to fulfill James 1:27: "look after orphans."

b. More and more churches now are encouraging families to adopt or to take temporary care of children. Churches should be in touch with local agencies who are involved with such work so that they can provide information to families about assisting with needy children. Those who are providing such assistance enjoy spending time together to share their struggles and successes.

c. Some churches have special days during which food and clothing are distributed. They advertise or share on social media, for example that on a specific day, they will be open to help those in need. They have items out where they may be easily inspected and allow people to collect a sack of groceries and a specified number of clothing items. They usually hold such an event in the church building or an auxiliary facility so that those coming will connect what they get with the church. They usually also have information about the church to hand out and, perhaps, the first lesson of a correspondence course. Some churches even collect the name and address of those who come so they can make additional contact. These days can become quite well-known and well-attended and, with good follow-up, can provide opportunities to set up Bible studies. One congregation in Branson, Missouri, makes meeting such physical needs its primary method of outreach and is quite successful in bringing to Christ those they serve.

d. Another organized effort can be providing "back-to-school" supplies. This can take two forms. Usually the church will have backpacks loaded with folders, pencils, notebooks, and other things which various grade levels will need as the school year begins. Sometimes the student is required to purchase certain textbooks for a particular grade level, so the church provides those, too. The church may even provide a winter coat or a required uniform. A second form of "back-to-school" serving may be to help teachers. Sometimes schools do not provide all the things teachers will need for their work in the

HOW THE BENEVOLENCE PROGRAM *Can be its Best*

classroom, and churches can help with these. One church even has the teachers from a nearby school to its building for a lunch on one of the days they are in pre-school activities. In all these cases, churches create goodwill and have an opportunity for follow-up with those they help.

6. **Another method for helping local schools is to provide tutors for students who are falling behind and sponsors for school trips.** Sometimes schools like to have a homeroom helper. A church can contact the principal in a nearby school to see how they can be of the most help.

7. **Churches also sometimes have special events connected with benevolence.**
    a. A church might do something special for Thanksgiving such as a plan for providing a meal of turkey and all the trimmings to people with special needs. They may serve the meal at their building so that people make a strong connection between the meal and the church. Others take the meal to homes of the poor, to a center where the poor are staying, and even to firemen, policemen, and others who are on duty and cannot be home on the holiday. Such an effort requires careful planning. Members may bring some of the food already cooked, or they can provide money to purchase items for members to prepare in the church kitchen.
    b. At Christmas time, a congregation could provide boxes of gifts appropriate for various age levels and then make these available by setting a day when poorer people can come to the building to select an appropriate box. They could also have coats available for those who need them. Other churches provide members the opportunity to pick up a list of things needed by individuals in a poor area with whom they have contact, and church members purchase gifts for a known child. The church then sends or gives the box or other material to that person. Some churches have contact with a church in Mexico or other country where a local congregation has many poor people attending, and they prepare boxes to be sent to that congregation, which distributes them. Sometimes these are called Magi boxes.

c. As strange as it may seem, many churches now participate in Halloween with an event called "Trunk or Treat." In this case, on the day when children will be going from house to house or on some other evening near that time, members come with items to distribute from the trunk of their car. Children, often with their parents, go from trunk to trunk to pick up treats. By providing such an event in the church parking lot, non-church families are drawn to the building for this activity and form a good opinion of the church.

8. **Churches may have a benevolence center.** Several churches can contribute supplies of food and clothing for a "warehouse" located where many poor people live. Someone, of course, needs to be designated to oversee the operation. This person or ones he could designate would be available when the center is open. Some churches would need to have the center in their budget to cover the expenses of building upkeep and perhaps a salary for the manager.

    This large area would have tables where clothing is already sorted so people can look for their specific need and size. Canned goods and other non-perishable items also are sorted and placed on tables. Assisting churches can occasionally send a group to help sort clothing, arrange other items, and help with keeping the facility in good condition.

    This center is open every day or at designated times, and the people in the community learn these times. One church in a rather poor community has such a center to which other congregations contribute money and supplies. Their major local evangelism outreach is connected with this work. They provide correspondence courses and other information to those who come and often set up studies. Through this plan, they convert several each year who then become connected with the local church.

9. **In some larger cities, there may be an inner-city where many poor live.** Some congregations have established congregations there, which provide for many needs of those in the area. First of all, they are there to help them learn about the gospel and to provide a place where they can attend the assembly. Some have the Sunday service at 4 p.m. so those from supporting congregations can attend their own congregation in

the morning and help with the inner-city church in the afternoon. They hold classes at 5 p.m. and after that provide a meal for all who have come.

Often on Sunday afternoons and on some other evening of the week, they will provide a free medical clinic using doctors, nurses, pharmacists, and perhaps translators who volunteer their services. Those who come to the clinic in the facility where there church meets are fully aware that the church is providing this service. This congregation can also provide food and clothing, and it is good if those receiving medical help are the same ones who receive other services. Such a plan means that these who are receiving these services become more closely connected with the church and, thus, more likely to be willing to have a home study.

Those interested in the possibility of considering an inner-city work should contact those who have such a facility in Oklahoma City, Tulsa, Little Rock, Ft. Worth, Nashville, Memphis, and many other places. For information on inner city ministry opportunities in your area, simply enter "inner city ministry, churches of Christ" and the name of your city in the web browser of your choice.

Every church should have a strong benevolence program to help its own members and those from outside the church. Churches should be teaching members, and even children, how to help others, so they will do this as individuals. And, of course, they should have good activities that the church plans and supports for which members can work together. The Lord certainly gave benevolent work a high priority, and so should we.

CHAPTER 9

 **THE YOUTH MINISTRY**

Can be its Best

Sixty years ago, few churches had special programs for youth. They had a Bible class for teens, and there were a few camps where young people could go during the summer. Some churches had occasional youth activities, but not many had any one called a "youth minister." Since that time, nearly all churches, except some pretty small ones, try to give special attention to the teenagers.

Still, those who study the youth coming from churches of all types say that 60-70 percent of them leave the church in which they grew up. Various reasons are given for this and with some validity. One study says that churches do not involve young people sufficiently in the work of the church—they do not use them to help lead worship, they do not involve them in benevolence work, they do not involve them in upkeep of the building, and on down the list. Other studies suggest that the problem is in the home. Parents have turned over the spiritual development of the children to the youth program and have neglected it at home. Thus, the children do not recognize the importance of staying faithful to the church. Still others suggest that the youth classes do not teach the fundamentals of the faith. They deal with some useful topics, but do not teach the young people about the basic truths of Scripture, the differences among churches, or the difference between the teaching of Scripture and the teaching of culture. Thus, they leave a blank spot in the training of the young people.

All of these things suggest that there must be a well-conceived youth program, so families and churches together may "train up a child in the way he should go, even when he is old he will not depart from it" (Proverbs 22:6, ESV). The New Testament gives a similar admonition: "bring up [your children] in the training and instruction of the Lord" (Ephesians 6:4, NIV). Jesus taught little children, and Paul mentions that Timothy's mother and grandmother had taught him "from infancy" (2 Timothy 1:4; 3:14-5). John makes an interesting statement about his children when speaking of his children in the Lord: "I have no greater joy than to hear that my children are walking in the truth" (3 John 4, NIV).

The following are some points on which those responsible for the youth program can check themselves to see if they can find ways to improve their program.

1. **Teach and motivate parents to carry out their spiritual responsibility to their children.** Your congregation can have a class for parents about their responsibility. For some information on one way to conduct such a class, go to *mrcc.org/spfc* to find a handbook with the information needed to teach the class as well as lesson plans about how to structure and teach the class sessions. Occasionally an elder can encourage parents to give major attention to training their children spiritually by doing such things as memorizing Scripture, being able to explain the meaning of key passages about Christian living, praying, and making good decisions. The preacher can bring sermons that encourage families to be what they should be: parents to train their children, children to work with them, families to serve the Lord together. The church can and should have good education programs from babies through teens, but the major responsibility lies with the parents, who must be taught how to teach their children at home.

2. **Have outstanding classes for youth.** There are three elements that will make classes for teens what they should be:

    (1) the topics should be chosen to teach both the fundamentals of the faith and to encourage Christian living;

    (2) the teaching methods should be well-adapted for teens (more later);

(3) the classes need to encourage activities that will bond together the students with the teacher and others involved in the program—youth minister, elders, preacher, and parents. Below is a list of objectives those planning classes should use as a basis for determining what the youth should study. Other objectives may certainly be added, but using these should provide the core of the program. Special classes should be developed to reach a set of these objectives, but the teacher of a class on a Bible book such as Acts, for example, should review the objectives to see which ones could be reached through the study of that book.

  a. Can explain the plan of salvation and encourage someone to obey it.

  b. Can state the case for the existence of God.

  c. Can state the case for the Bible as an infallible revelation inspired by God and as the authority for Christian faith and practice.

  d. Can use the principles of hermeneutics to determine the meaning of Bible passages.

  e. Can state the case for the divinity of Christ.

  f. Can explain the nature of the church as the saved, the body of Christ and that the church is not a denomination.

  g. Can trace the predictions and the history of the departure from Christ's original plan for the church as revealed in the New Testament, the efforts of the Reformation Movement to move back in that direction, and then the efforts to restore the New Testament plan for the teaching and practice of the church.

  h. Can provide reasons from Scripture as to why churches of Christ do not use instruments with their singing.

  i. Can provide reasons from Scripture as to why in churches of Christ only men lead in worship.

  j. Can use the Sermon on the Mount, the list of Christian graces, and the list of the fruits of the Spirit to describe Christ-like character and will demonstrate such qualities in his/her personal life.

  k. Can trace the story of God's plan for saving sinful people starting with the sin of Adam through God's choice of Abraham to build a family, God's work through the nation of Israel both to provide a Messiah and to demonstrate that a person cannot keep the law to perfection, to the coming of Christ and His undeserved death, and finally the establishment of the church as the fulfillment of God's plan.

   l. Can state the case for creation as opposed to evolution.

   m. Can properly use helps for Bible study such as a concordance, Bible dictionary, commentaries, and the internet.

   n. Can participate in worship in a meaningful and scriptural way.

   o. Can tell how a Christian would respond to various situations involving moral decisions.

   p. Can explain God's plan for marriage, divorce, and re-marriage.

   q. Will use relationships with others such as neighbors or fellow-workers as opportunities to bring people to Christ.

   r. Will submit to parents, elders, and others in positions of authority.

   s. Will be regular in attendance at Sunday worship and Bible study times.

   t. Will actively be engaged in serving such as helping others, working in church ministries, speaking with friends, and inviting them to attend or to have a Bible study.

3. **Teaching methods for classes should include brief lecture, class discussion of the topic, and opportunities for the class to make practical application of the lesson.** No lesson should be without specific application to the lives of teens. This means that the teacher should often be saying "So when you….," or asking the class "What if you were….?" Some churches find it helpful to have a 15-minute lesson in youth classes and then to break the class into groups of six or eight with an older person or couple to lead the small group. This allows not only discussion of the topic and its applications to real life, but it also connects the young people to a person of a different generation, which is a vitally important thing to do.

4. **Classes for teens should include what the Bible teaches about current issues** such as why bad things happen to good people, race relations, homosexuality, treatment of people with differing political views, dealing with people who come here from different countries, evolution,

and the teaching of the Bible on absolutes such as moral truths Christians are to follow.

5. **Teen retreats can be greatly beneficial.** These may be for the young men, for the young women, or for all the youth. The events can be held at a youth camp, at a public facility like a state park, or as a sleep over at the church building. These retreats should include good instruction, devotionals, time for reflection, and recreational activities when the kids can play together. The aims should be for the teens to learn more about Bible teaching on important topics, to help them establish important spiritual goals, to increase their level of spiritual commitment, and to give them stronger fellowship within the group.

6. **Summer camps are also important activities for youth.** These may be with just the youth of your congregation or may be combined with youth of other congregations. These longer times away seek not only to help them increase their knowledge of the Bible, but also to provide the occasion for them to make important commitments and to develop stronger friendships. When things young people like to do are placed within a spiritual context, it has important benefits. These might even become the times when some will decide to be baptized, when some will decide to become missionaries or preachers, make moral commitments, or make important decisions about the type of person they want to marry.

7. **There should be many opportunities for serving.** Since the youth of today especially like to serve people, the youth program should find ways to involve the them in good works. Some of this service should be church-related in the sense that the youth carry out projects that help the church. They can, for example, help with workdays at the church to make improvements around the building and in the yard. They can go door-to-door to advertise an upcoming event such as a special seminar at the church or VBS. They can help welcome visitors to the services. Think of the great impression a visitor would have in being greeted at the door by a teen member of the church.

The youth should also help with community projects the church can do—cleaning a stretch of road, helping with a church booth at the county fair, clearing the snow from sidewalks and driveways, helping with a widow's yard, going to sing for a shut-in, and other things the church may decide to do. Sometimes these projects can be done just by the youth group and sometimes they can work alongside older members. Such inter-generational contact is highly valuable. One of the primary reasons we lose youth after they are out on their own is because they did not feel included, needed, or connected with the older members. We must train them and utilize them in good ways while they are in their teen years.

8. **After the young men have been well trained, they should be involved in leading the worship**—serving the Lord's Supper, praying, leading singing, reading Scripture, and maybe bringing the message on occasional Sunday nights. It is important for the church to see its youth assisting with the services as well as being important for the young men to be getting that experience and that involvement.

9. **The youth can be involved in mission trips, just among themselves or mixed with older people in the congregation.** Some of the most memorable events in a young person's life could be a mission trip to Haiti or to Honduras or to some place in the United States. One of the most important features of such trips is the intense preparation for these events, which sometimes involves memorizing Scriptures, helping those going to be prepared to teach people the Bible, lessons on the culture they will find, and helping them to know about the churches where they will be going.

Properly training our youth to be the church of tomorrow is essential. The church is always just a generation from extinction. For the good of the church and the importance of the souls of the youth, we must have strong programs to teach and to utilize our young people.

CHAPTER 10

HOW THE WOMEN'S MINISTRY
Can be its Best

God has always used women as a key part of His plan. Just think of Sarah, Rachael, Ruth, Elizabeth, Mary, Mary Magdalene, and Priscilla. Likewise, Christ has an important place for women in the church today. In some respects, it is different from the role of men, but no less important. Paul makes it clear in 1 Corinthians 11:3 that the order of authority is God, Christ, man, woman, so men are to lead in the public worship (1 Corinthians 14:33-34), and men are to be the elders of the church (1 Timothy 3:2). Women, however, have key roles to play in their families and in the life of the church.

Note these passages that speak of the work of women.

- To be clothed in "good works"—1 Timothy 2:10.
- To train younger women to love their husbands and children and to be workers at home—Titus 2:4-5.
- To bring up children, to show hospitality, to wash the saints feet, to relieve the afflicted, to follow diligently every good work—1 Timothy 5:9-10.
- To be involved in private teaching—Acts 18:26.

Many outstanding ministries in congregations have begun at the initiative of women. Many works in benevolence, education, local outreach, and missions have come from the encouragement women have given. There are a host of wonderful works for them to do in the home and in the church. Their work is as important to God and to the church as anything men do. It is just different in some respects.

Let me depart from the usual plan of these chapters to use Jo Anne, my wife of 64 years, as an example of what women can do because I believe her story can inspire many. We were married when she was 20 and I was 25. At the time, I was preaching for a church of about 250 in Gainesville, Florida. She immediately dove into the work of being a minister's wife. She visited homes and hospitals with me, she taught children's classes, she sang in a church choral group that went to nursing homes and hospitals, and she was hospitable—even having guests for breakfast our first day home from our honeymoon. She taught in VBS and helped me publish the weekly church bulletin. All the while, she was going to school full-time to complete her bachelor's degree in business education.

In 1956 we moved to Bartlesville, Oklahoma, where I taught at Central Christian College. She had guests to the duplex where we lived, was involved in activities at the college, and taught a class in swimming. We drove every Sunday to places where I would preach, and she would greet people and take care of our son. In 1958 the college moved to Oklahoma City and later became Oklahoma Christian University. From 1958 until 1965, I was the regular preacher every Sunday at Guthrie, about 20 miles from where we lived, and our family had grown to include four children. She was with me every Sunday—greeting, helping me know people's needs, going with me on personal visits and Bible studies, teaching children's classes, and spending Sunday afternoon with the kids in the home of whoever invited us to Sunday dinner—nice but no small chore.

In 1965, we placed membership with the College Church, now Memorial Road, and had many people to our home—couples, class groups of 30-40, and every year for 25 years, we had all the employees at Oklahoma Christian and their families to our backyard for a July 4th party with the number sometimes as high as 180. For this event, Jo Anne prepared much of the food and was a great hostess.

She taught pre-school classes at Memorial Road, and for a time, she was the director of the pre-school program there. For several years she taught the sixth grade class about Bible lands and later taught them with a program she developed for students to use a computer in the classroom to learn about the Bible. She wrote a set of lessons for Vacation Bible School, which was published and used widely. For many years, she taught a women's Bible class and was the coordinator of the women's program at Memorial Road. For more than 30 years, she has stood with me at the back of the auditorium to bless members and guests as they leave. At Oklahoma Christian, she taught classes in reading improvement and in teaching Bible classes to elementary and pre-school children.

In the fall of 1983, Jo Anne started the prison work at the Memorial Road Church of Christ which has become one of the most successful prison works in the brotherhood. During all of those years, she has taught classes of women in prison and gone to the county jail to teach women one-on-one. When women have been released from prison, she has kept several in our home for a few days or as long as three months. She sends a baptismal card to all who are baptized through the prison work, which may be as many as 15 a month, and she goes to the jail once a month to be there when people she and others have taught that month are baptized. She also sends cards to all those baptized at the church, and her card ministry also includes sympathy cards when a member has lost a loved one or someone is in the hospital.

In addition, she has gone on many mission trips where she has taught women's classes, done door-to-door work, taught one-on-one, and counseled the wives of missionaries. These trips include visits to Poland, India, Guatemala, two to England, three to Brazil, two to Nigeria, and three to Kenya. She also helped to lead five groups to learn about the Bible as people toured the Bible lands.

All the while, Jo Anne was helping to raise four children who have had 10 grandchildren and so far have provided us with 17 great-grandchildren. She also sends cards and gifts on their birthday to every one of the 44 now in the clan and, of course, she sends presents to all at Christmas. For several years, she had Mama Jo's Memory Verse Club through which she sent verses each month for the older great-grandchildren to memorize and to recite at our yearly gathering at the beach, which she also initiated. At 84, she has slowed down a bit, but still goes to teach women in the jail, has people to our home for meals, visits the hospitals and in homes, and continues her card ministry. And, oh yes, since 1972, she has been

HOW THE WOMEN'S MINISTRY *Can be its Best*

supporting me as an elder's wife and all that goes with that.

The point of this story is that there are great things for women to do that are just as important as the work men do and from which they can get the great satisfaction of serving the Lord's kingdom.

Now to the list for a women's program at the church. Every congregation needs someone or some group to plan the activities and the work of the women. **A wise selection from the good things mentioned below will not happen unless someone is directly charged with planning and executing those items most suitable in a particular congregation.**

1. **A women's Bible study, typically on a Wednesday or Thursday morning.**

   In some larger congregations, there is also an evening, noon, or an early morning Bible study for women who work or whose responsibilities for children make them unavailable during the day. These studies should be chosen to help women grow in their understanding of Scripture and in the applications they should make to their own lives. One of the most interesting stories I have heard about such a Bible study happened in Nigeria when my wife and I were there teaching for a short period of time. A woman was converted through a Bible study, but her husband was not pleased with this and forbade her to attend church. She did, however, go to a daytime Bible study my wife was teaching, which dealt with how women should be good wives. She taught them to be like "a pillow" and "not a rock." For the next few days, the woman practiced what she had been taught to be like a pillow, and her husband noticed the difference. He asked her one day, "What has made you so different?" She told him it was becoming a Christian and learning how to be a good wife. He said to her, "If going to church has made this difference in you, you can go every time."

   So women's studies should help women know the Bible, but also should help them in their family responsibilities and to know how to serve the Lord. Some good topics for these studies are:

   a. particular books of the Bible,

   b. women of the Bible,

   c. women's role in the church,

   d. women's role as wife and mother,

e. the Christian graces, and

   f. how to reach others for Christ.

   When selected materials are written by someone who holds different beliefs than the church in which the classes are being held, these differences should be discussed and used as a point of teaching what the Bible says on these points. Sometimes these classes have monthly luncheons following their studies to give women a time for fellowship.

2. **Some congregations have small group Bible studies for women as part of their Wednesday night Bible school programs or at other appropriate times.** Such sessions can help women become better connected with others, give them a chance to learn together, allow them to discuss questions they have, share with others about special needs, and have prayer time together. Small groups like this can be beneficial because they allow women to discuss freely among themselves. The leaders of such groups need to know how not only to lead in a study of the Bible, but also how to help women use the Scriptures in dealing with problems or issues they may have. If there are several such groups, it can be helpful for the leaders of these groups to meet together prior to the time when they will be studying a passage or a topic to help one another be well-prepared for leading the group.

3. **A weekend retreat for women can be a great time of fellowship and building relationships as well as a time for study and devotion.**

4. **A special study could be held on a Saturday to teach older women how to mentor the younger women.** Then a follow-up session could provide the opportunity for connecting the older women with younger ones to allow for such mentoring to be done. Heartfelt Ministries has a plan for doing this, which one can access at *heartfeltministries.org*.

5. **Women should be active in teaching classes for children.** They could attend classes at the level of their interest to learn about both the content of the lessons they will teach and methods they can use.

6. **Experienced teachers should make it their goal to bring other women into the educational program.** They can discover those whom they believe would do well and to make the effort to encourage them to teach and then to take them under their wing to mentor them.

7. **The women's program could provide many opportunities for women through special events such as:**
   a. an author coming to review her good book about something of special benefit to women,
   b. a class to encourage and teach mothers,
   c. a seminar on how to be a good wife, and
   d. a session on special qualities which women should seek to develop in their lives. Such sessions not only provide useful instruction, but offer opportunities for fellowship among the women, which may develop into continuing friendships. Some congregations have a dinner for the women prior to the presentation.
8. **Have events that take women in small groups to go to three or four homes in an evening to enjoy fellowship and to study briefly at each stop.**
9. **Some churches have a "boxes" class by which they seek to contact women who have recently moved to the community and are still unpacking their boxes.** Through a series of weekly meetings at the church building, those from the church who are leading in this class seek to do things to acquaint the new person in the community with many things they need to know about where and how to get things done. They also spend some time in helping those attending to know something about what their church does to serve people and, thus, to attract them to want to come to the church. Those interested can have special Bible studies. Through such a program, the church builds good will among those in the community and also will find some who learn about the church and want to become members.
10. **Women can volunteer to serve in important ways as suggested below, and the church should make women aware of such opportunities.** A woman may do her work individually or in partnership with a friend, or in a group carrying out one or more of these activities:
    a. Grade correspondence courses in jail/prison work or in something like World Bible Study.
    b. Visit those women who are elderly, who are ill at home, who are in the hospital, or who live alone and need friends.

c. Reach out to those who are recent converts or who are new to the congregation. Call, send cards, take them out to lunch, or go to see them at their home.

d. Greet people at the door when they enter the church building to attend a service, paying particular attention to those who are visiting. This could include helping to serve at a visitor's center if the church has one in the lobby.

e. Follow up with those who have visited the church services by sending them cards, reaching out to them by phone, or by going to their home. Showing this interest can help them decide to come back again.

f. Contact people who are falling away from the church and seek to rescue them.

g. Note those women at church who are struggling with problems at home or who need encouragement and help them.

h. Encourage those who have lost a loved one by calling, visiting or even by taking a cake or pie to the home of the bereaved. Make a special effort to attend the funeral of anyone from the congregation to provide support for those suffering a loss.

i. Connect with one or two children at church who need an older woman in their life and to treat them as "grandchildren," sitting with them in church and having them to your home.

j. Go on a mission trip to teach children and women, to help with construction projects, to assist with medical clinics, to encourage the missionaries, and to serve in other ways.

k. Work with the school where your children attend to be a tutor, a chaperone, a teacher's helper, or be involved in the PTA. Such service not only helps the school and the children there, but opens doors for building good will for the church and making contacts, which can result in Bible studies.

l. Volunteer to work with the church office to answer the phone, to greet visitors, and to provide services to others.

m. Encourage your husband in his work at the church whether that is teaching, serving as an elder or deacon, or in some other ministry.

n. Use email and video conferencing tools to keep in touch with a missionaries and wives supported by the church to encourage them in their work.
o. Help make things needed in the pre-school and elementary programs at church—posters, crafts, visual aids.
p. Drive people who can't drive to their appointment with doctors or to get their groceries.
q. Work in the benevolence ministry to keep the clothing and food panty in good order and to assist those who need help. You could also be part of a quilting group to make quilts to distribute to those who need them.
r. Help clean the church, care for flower beds, or assist with keeping bulletin boards current.
s. Help an inner-city work or a community help center by assisting in many ways: teaching a children's class, helping to prepare meals, organizing the clothing and food for distribution, or assisting with a medical clinic.
t. Work with VBS at the church. You could also host a backyard VBS at your home for neighborhood children. Children are often looking for something to do during the summer and so are their parents. To have a VBS in your backyard on several mornings in a row or one day a week for several weeks can do good by teaching the Bible and can also make contacts, which might lead a child to come to Bible classes at church or to bring a family to be interested in having a Bible study.
u. Help with the "back-to-school" program that the church may have.
v. Host parties at your home where people play games and enjoy fellowship, maybe for women only or for couples.
w. Make a special effort to know your neighbors by warmly greeting anyone who moves into your neighborhood and by visiting neighbors to invite them to your home for coffee in an effort to make youself the one available when they need a ride, are ill, or lose a loved one.
x. Give showers for those getting married or having babies and attend showers given by others. These occasions encourage others at the special times in their lives and help those getting married or having babies to appreciate those in the church.

y. Take care of baptismal clothing and towels by washing them and returning them for use.

z. Help those church members or visitors from other countries by teaching them about the Bible by studying English with them. Find a set of studies that uses the Book of Luke to help a person learn English using the Bible as the subject to read and discuss. In the process, many come to have a special interest in the content of the Bible and eventually become Christians.

The list could go on, but these should be enough to give ideas both to individuals and groups studying the work of the women in your congregation. These suggestions run the gamut from individual to group projects. Having strong involvement of women in the work of the local congregation is essential, and many congregations need to do more to find good ways to capture the contributions women make to their program. The church can provide women with many beneficial activities and should continue to seek ways to maximize what women can do for the church.

As Paul closes his epistle to the Romans, he mentions two women who have been especially good workers in the church. "I commend to you our sister Phoebe, a servant of the church in Cenchrea, that you may welcome her in the Lord in a way worthy of the saints, and help her helping whatever she may need from you, for she has been a patron of many and of myself as well. Greet Priscilla and Aquila, my fellow workers in Christ Jesus, who risked their necks for my life, to whom not only I give thanks but all the churches of the Gentiles give thanks as well. Greet also the church in their house" (Romans 16:1-5, ESV). There are many great women in the church today and may God help churches to find the best way to serve them and to utilize them.

CHAPTER 11

HOW THE MEN'S MINISTRY

Can be its Best

A men's ministry can bring many important benefits both to men's personal lives and to the congregation of which they are a part. Paul's first letter to Timothy outlines some excellent directions for which men should strive. Although Timothy was a young preacher, much of what Paul says to him applies to all men, regardless of their age, and these principles can guide in the development of a ministry for men.

In 1 Timothy 2:1 Paul urges that "petitions, prayers, intercession and thanksgiving be made for all people" (NIV). A vital part of a men's ministry should be to help men to be prayerful, as individuals, as leaders in the church, and as leaders of their homes. In 1 Timothy 4:7, Paul urges Timothy to train himself to be godly, so a men's ministry should help men to be God-like in their lives, to be men who seek to be holy and moral.

First Timothy 4:10 speaks of "hope in the living God," suggesting how important it is for Christians to be filled with hope. So a men's ministry should anchor men in hope. In 4:12, Paul urges Timothy to set an example for the believers "in speech, in conduct, in love, in faith, [and] in purity" (ESV). There could hardly be found anywhere a better description of the life toward which men should strive. In 4:14, Paul tells Timothy not to neglect the gift he had received. His was likely a miraculous gift of some type, but for us today, this passage is an admonition to use the talents we have for the Lord. In 4:16, Paul tells Timothy to watch closely "his life" and "his doctrine" (NIV). We need men who are sound in life and in doctrine. In 6:6, Paul tells Timothy that "godliness with contentment is great gain" and goes on to warn that people who want to get rich fall into a temptation and a trap that will lead to ruin and destruction. Men must be warned not to make riches their goal in life. And finally, in 6:11, Paul tells Timothy to pursue righteousness, godliness, faith, love, endurance, and gentleness and to fight the good fight of faith.

So, from these passages in which Paul teaches Timothy, we can draw the following goals for a men's ministry. A man should be prayerful, godly, hopeful, a good example, using his gift, watching his life and doctrine, not a lover of money, and one who has the personal qualities of faith, love, gentleness, and endurance. A man who has attained a good level in these matters will be a good husband, father, employee, worker in the church, and will have the personal qualities to let his light shine. So, as those who do the planning for a men's ministry go about their work, they should keep these admonitions in mind. Their classes for men, their small groups, and their special events should all work toward helping men to be what Paul wanted Timothy to be.

Now to some specifics about what a men's ministry can do

1. **The ministry needs good leadership through a director who has a good committee working with him.** They need to be active in planning the events they want to use to help men of the congregation to grow spiritually. The elders, of course, should oversee this work to be sure that it is achieving its desired ends.

2. **The ministry must do a good job of selling itself to the men of the congregation, so they will participate in their programs.** They will need a list of the men in the congregation by email addresses to be able to send information directly to them. Although public announcements will be helpful, a more direct individual contact is needed. They can also have some key participants in their activities who will each have a list of men with whom he can work by direct contact through seeing them personally and calling or texting them by phone.

3. **The ministry can have a men's Bible class that meets either one evening a week or in some other pattern such as two Saturday mornings a month.** This class can study subjects to help men grow in their knowledge of

Scripture and in their growth toward the type of men whom Paul taught Timothy to be. If the congregation is large enough, there could be enough older men in the congregation who would not be going to work and could meet on a Wednesday or Thursday morning.

4. **A men's retreat once or twice a year can achieve good results.** On a Friday night and Saturday, men can go to a site where they can spend the night for Bible study, fellowship, and private prayer. The location could be a camp, a hotel, or even the local church building (in which case they would probably go home after the evening session and be back the next morning). Well-planned events that are modest in price can draw a good group. The speakers and group leaders can come from the congregation, but bringing in an outside speaker, particularly a person known to the men as being effective, will likely draw more of them to come.

5. **A men's breakfast can be an excellent element in the men's program.** Such a breakfast can be once a week, twice a month, or monthly. These events can be at the church building, and some men should offer to do the cooking. The breakfast can be a time of getting to know one another better as well as a time of prayer and an opportunity to study a quality topic toward which all should strive or a time to push an activity in which all should participate. Another good thing to do with the breakfast meetings is occasionally to invite men from another congregation to come. These invitations could include men from a congregation that is predominately of a different race or background. Such occasions can build good relationships with those who have not had much contact in the past.

6. **The Wednesday evening schedule, when most congregations have Bible classes, is another opportunity for men's classes.** These could last for a quarter and deal with topics to help achieve the qualities listed from 1 Timothy. There are also study guides written just for men's classes that could be useful. Another opportunity Wednesday night classes could provide is for men to meet in smaller discussion groups, which may provide ample opportunities for men to be more open with one another about their struggles and needs. These sessions could offer the

opportunity for two men to agree to work together as accountability partners with each one indicating that he will be available for a call or a meeting anytime he is needed to help his partner hold fast or discuss a matter. These classes can also teach the importance of faithfulness in marriage, how to be a good partner, and message from Scripture for marriage to last a lifetime. Men should be deeply grounded in their commitment to their wives and how to keep a marriage everlasting. (Yes, everlasting.)

7. **The men's ministry can also bring in special speakers to deal with men's issues for an early morning, Saturday, or evening event.** Men can invite their non-member friends to such occasions. Thus these sessions can not only be good for spiritual development among the men, but a good opportunity for evangelism.

8. **Another opportunity for the men's ministry is to plan events involving both the husband and wife.** Some churches, for example, have a special event at a hotel where someone can speak at a banquet setting and then the couples have time for themselves. This plan offers another way to encourage faithfulness and strengthen relationships between men and their wives.

9. **The men's ministry can help men to be involved in ministries at church such as local evangelism, building and grounds, missions, benevolence, education, and others.** The ministry can encourage them to connect with a ministry and can help them to get involved by a ministry fair. Thus the ministry helps men to fulfill their calling from the Lord by utilizing their talents.

10. **The men's ministry can provide a mentoring program, which matches more mature men with younger ones.** The two partners could meet for breakfast or lunch once a month to discuss having a strong marriage, being a good father, serving in the church, taking part in the men's activities, and problems or needs the younger man might have.

11. **The men's ministry can also encourage and assist men to serve in ways that will connect them with one another and with the community.**

    a. Men can be involved with one another and in good work through a workday planned by the men's ministry. This could be a time when the focus is on improvements and cleanup of the church building and the grounds around it. The men could also break into smaller groups and go to local schools, city playgrounds, or the homes of widows and elderly folks to do things there that need to be done. Good planning should precede these events to be sure that someone knows exactly what needs to be done at each place and to be certain that the right tools are assembled. These workdays have a triple opportunity for good:

(1) They achieve the improvements that need to be made;

(2) They give men a time of growing closer to one another; and

(3) They give men a chance to invite friends who are not members of the church to do something with their church friends. Often a person who is not yet ready to come to church with a friend will come to a workday, and that is a terrific start.

b. Men can also be engaged through sports. The ministry can encourage men to coach a little league team, which gives them the opportunity to show the young players, the opposing team, and the parents attending how a Christian acts at a sporting event. Through this activity, he can have the opportunity to invite the young men to VBS or some other church event. And, having established a good relationship with parents, he can invite them to special church events as well.

If the men have access to a gym at the church building or elsewhere, they can have a basketball league for teams that wish to compete. These can be both for teens and for adults. And again, this gives the opportunity for all those involved to see how Christians compete. Starting with a brief prayer before the game and ending with a short devotional after the game can show others where your hearts are—with God, not with winning!. When we let our light shine, we attract people to want to know more about us, and we bring glory to God.

Men may also connect with a high school or college sports team in the area to serve as a "chaplain," or if that title does not work, just to be a helper like a "father figure" for the team. In this role, they can counsel, advise, and assist players who are having a problem. They might even tutor an athlete in a school subject with which he is having trouble. Such connections can help him broaden his sphere of influence.

Some churches have a golf tournament each year to which men are encouraged to invite a friend. The church member pays for the round of golf and a little more and the friend comes free. The group can either start with breakfast or end with lunch at which time the local preacher or some other person from the church makes a few comments and invites the friends to visit the church services or some special event.

c. Other types of activities of the men's ministry can also give the opportunity to serve. If the church is in a farming area, for example, the men can work with FFA or other similar groups, they can have a booth for the church at a county fair, they can also work to help someone who needs assistance by plowing, planting, or harvesting a crop. Or if there has been a disaster in the area, they can work together to help those who have suffered losses.

So, a well-organized and well-planned men's ministry can do good in so many ways. It can help the men of the congregation grow in spiritual insights and Bible knowledge. It can help them to be more prayerful and to develop in Christian qualities. It can strengthen them through fellowship and by assisting them in using their talents for the Lord. It can help their roles as husbands and fathers and can train them for roles of leadership in the church. Every church needs to have some of the elements mentioned above in its program as it seeks to help its members "grow in the grace and knowledge of our Lord" (2 Peter 3:18, NIV).

CHAPTER 12

THE MINISTRY FOR YOUNG ADULTS
Can be its Best

Paul wrote three of his 13 letters to young adults—two to Timothy and one to Titus. He knew the importance of helping these men to be useful and faithful. To them he wrote such things as "fight the battle well, holding on to faith and a good conscience" (1 Timothy 1:18-19, NIV); "train yourself to be godly. For physical training is of some value, but godliness has value for all things, holding promise for both the present life and the life to come" (1 Timothy 4:7-8); "set an example for the believers in speech, in conduct, in love, in faith, and in purity" (1 Timothy 4:12, NIV); "Watch your life and doctrine closely" (1 Timothy 4:16, NIV); "Treat younger men as brothers, older women as mothers, and younger women as sisters, with absolute purity" (1 Timothy 5:1-2, NIV)); "Those who want to get rich fall into temptation and a trap and into many foolish and harmful desires that plunge men into ruin and destruction" (1 Timothy 6:9, NIV); "Take hold of the eternal life to which you were called" (1 Timothy 6:12, NIV); "... fan into flame the gift of God, which is in you" (2 Timothy 1:6, NIV); "do not be ashamed of the testimony about our Lord" (2 Timothy 1:8, ESV); "say 'No' to ungodliness and worldly passions, and to live self-controlled, upright and godly lives" (Titus 2:12, NIV); "be peaceable and considerate, and always to be gentle toward everyone" (Titus 3:2, NIV).

Though Paul was writing to young men, these admonitions apply to young women as well. In the section below, we will suggest things to teach young adults both married and single. This period, from college years through their 20s and for some even longer, is crucial. It is the time when many who have been taught to be Christians in their homes turn away from the faith. If a congregation loses its people of this age, it will likely lose its future. To that end, give some thought to the list below in an effort to strengthen your young adults in the faith.

1. **Help them set the right priorities.** Paul told Timothy to be godly and not to set his goal to be rich. While young men and women are in their 20s, they are setting the direction for their lives: choosing their profession, setting their lifestyle, and choosing a mate. It is easy for them to prioritize getting rich and having a position of importance as their goal whatever it takes, and they often decide that it takes living like the world. To combat these worldly goals, have a class that teaches about priorities, have group discussions that give them a chance to share, suggest books to read about what to do with your life, and have people of strong faith who have succeeded to associate with the young adults. Let them see how one can be godly and succeed, but that being godly is more important than being rich.

2. **Help them set their hope on heaven.** Paul said that godliness held a promise both for this life and the life to come. It is easy for young people to ignore "the life to come" by thinking that they have many years left to think about that. "I'm young. I'll enjoy all the pleasures of life I choose. I can be good later." Of course, some of them will not have "later," and others will set a course that will engulf them, and they will never change. Some at this point choose alcohol, drugs, and sex. These sins so entangle them that their lives are ruined forever, and so is their eternity. Help these young people see that the main thing in this life is to prepare for the next life. They may not have all the success now they've wished to have, and they may not have all the prominence they would like, but these are less important than hoping for heaven and preparing for it. Young people must be reminded that many who fall into sin find that what they have done has become a great obstacle both for this life and the life to come.

3. **Help them to watch their doctrine closely.** Paul repeatedly warns Timothy and Titus to be true to the faith and not to waver. Young

adults need to be deepened in their understanding of Scriptures and particularly need to be grounded in the fundamentals of the faith. They need to be prepared to "give an answer" to those around them who hold different beliefs. Studying doctrinal matters may not be their favorite topic, so it needs to be made challenging and interesting. Prepare them to answer doctrinal questions. Let someone in class take the position of some false teaching, and let others in the class defend the truth. Find statements in books that either favor or do not favor the teaching of Scripture, and let them examine the statement. Let them tell of conversations they are having with friends. Keep them grounded in the faith.

4. **Help them to live godly lives.** Paul often mentions the Christian qualities he wants Titus and Timothy to develop. They should be self-controlled, live a godly life, and "set an example in speech, in life, in love, in faith, and in purity." So the young adults need to know the personal qualities they should develop, and they need to have opportunities to discuss them. The world will tempt them to lie, cheat, steal, drink, take drugs, put others down so they can rise, and be involved in sexual immorality. What can keep them out of this? The teaching of Scripture, good examples both from others who are older and who are of their own age, and a study of cases in the public square of individuals who have ruined their life, their career, their marriage, and their own happiness by immoral conduct are all great examples. Many today, for example, are shamed out of public office because they have made unwanted advances to people sexually, have embezzled money, have cheated on their income taxes, or have made fools of themselves while under the influence of alcohol or drugs. Discuss such cases. Enable young adults to have accountability partners with whom they can share their temptations, to whom they can make promises, and whom they can contact when they are moving in the wrong direction.

Living such godly lives applies both to the married and unmarried young adults. The single ones should keep themselves pure, and so should the married ones. The single ones should be self-controlled, and so should the married ones. In a smaller church, these will be taught together, while in a larger church they will probably be in different classes. Even then, they still should have some contact with one another because they have much in common.

5. **Help them set a good example for one another.** Paul told Timothy to "set an example in speech, in conduct, in love, in faith, and in purity" (1 Timothy 4:12, NIV). This is a high calling. There is no doubt, however, that those young adults who follow a high standard will be an encouragement for others to do the same. As the group is broken into small groups for study and for discussion, some of those setting the best example should be scattered among the groups so that some on the edge are not the only ones in any group. Teach classes about the calling to be a good example in everything and how much this can help all the young adults to live better lives.

    It is good for young people to know that even though we live in a world where many are engaged in immoral behavior, most still appreciate a person who lives with good moral standards. The "boss" still appreciates those who tell the truth, who treat others with respect, and those who stay out of sinful sexual behavior. Some may joke about the one who does not drink or "party," but in the end, they actually respect those living by standards that keep them out of trouble. Often they will promote such a person before promoting the one who makes a fool of himself at the company Christmas party.

6. **Help them to be humble.** Paul called on Timothy to develop this trait, and it is a crucial one for young adults. Those who have early success will be tempted to be proud of what they have done, will fall into a snare, and will make others feel bad because they have achieved less. Classes should teach about the benefit of humility and show how Christ was humble even though He was God in the flesh.

7. **Help them see that whatever their status, they are OK.** It is good to be married, but the Lord also needs those who are single. Do not downgrade those not married. Jesus was single. Paul was single during the time of his life that we know about. Jesus even said that some are single "for the sake of the kingdom of heaven" (Matthew 19:12, NIV). You can, however, have events in which those not married can meet

other singles who can be friends. If those develop into something more, that is fine, but don't push such events in a way that downgrades being single.

8. **Help them use their talents for the Lord.** Paul told Timothy to "fan into flame" his gift. Even though Timothy may have had a miraculous gift, the principle is the same. Our talents or gifts may be used or may remain dormant, and young people need to fan their gift into flame. Paul also called on Timothy not to be ashamed to testify about our Lord.

    Young people today like to serve, and the church should take advantage of that. They can be encouraged to share their faith and to find something among the many ministries of the church in which to participate. As shown below, many opportunities of service need to be made available for young adults—sometimes working individually, sometimes with their group, and sometimes with those who are older. Occasionally, mixing the generations is important. Those who get involved in serving early in their lives are much more likely to remain faithful than those who never use their talents for the Lord.

    Get them active not only in ministry, but let them also serve on committees that help plan and oversee important work at the church. This service gives them useful involvement and also provides excellent training for future work. It also affords them a chance to have an important leading role, which will help them want to stay connected with the church.

Having seen the general qualities of life we should teach our young adults to acquire, here are some specific things those in charge of the work on young adults could do.

1. Have strong teachers for their classes who are great examples of what the young adults should want to be like. On occasion, at least, use people who have successful marriages for the married and people who are successful singles for the singles.
2. Have content for the classes that reflects what is mentioned above.
3. Have classes in which the older women teach the younger women and older men teach the younger men. They can study Bible topics and discuss many aspects of life.

4. Have classes and seminars on successful marriage for married and engaged couples.

5. Have classes or seminars on parenting for those who are reaching the point of having children.

6. Have retreats for singles and retreats for married couples and retreats where they are together. Young people enjoy getting away for things, so they should have a chance to escape to a retreat to study a Bible topic or a topic about their stage in life or have an opportunity for spiritual renewal through singing and praying and some time to meditate alone. Help them make a plan for their spiritual development and have an accountability partner to help them stay with the plan. Try to keep the cost of these events low, so those living on a tight budget can participate. Being together on retreats, trips, and other events gives the single young adults an opportunity to make friends and sometimes to find that often elusive significant other.

7. Have times when the young people get together to sing hymns in someone's home. Sometimes before singing the hymn, they can tell what that song means to them and why they suggested it.

8. Use small groups for the young adults. In these groups, they can do Bible study and share about things happening in their lives. It is good to have a mix of ages and of marital status in these small groups.

9. Take trips to other cities for sporting events, for suitable concerts, or to see a museum. The opportunity the group can have for visiting during the trip and to sense doing something together are both important. Such events will build the close ties the group needs.

10. Make a trip on a Sunday to visit a smaller congregation in the area. Plan with the smaller church for young men in your group to teach the Bible class and lead in the service. This will be an encouragement to the smaller congregation and a good growing opportunity for those who participate. Take food with you to feed both your group and the members of the congregation, and mix the seating so you can have "dinner" together and encourage one another.

11. Have mission trips in which the youth go to other places in the U.S. or even to foreign countries to help spread the gospel message.

Well-designed trips to such places as Haiti and Honduras can make a strong, positive spiritual impact on those who go as well as help the work in such places.

12. Sometimes events like those just mentioned can be done with singles from two or three or more congregations. These times together broaden the range of opportunities for friendships and even to meet someone of special interest.
13. Use young adults in leading the worship—on the Lord's Table, reading Scripture, leading prayers, and in making talks.
14. Ask young adults to help in greeting those who are coming through the entrance doors of the building. Also ask them to help in following up with visitors.
15. Use young adults in helping to keep the building and grounds in good shape. Have a work day, for example, as spring is coming on to plant flower and shrubs around the building.
16. If you have an inner-city work, that is a great place for young people to help teach and work with the disadvantaged youth.
17. Ask young adults to teach or to assist with children's classes. They can also help prepare the materials or crafts to be used in the classes.
18. Engage young adults to help with the church website and other computer needs.
19. Young adults can help with youth sporting events in which the church is encouraging in order to help children and teens develop good sportsmanship and to invite non-church friends to participate.
20. Use young adults to help with a meal for widows and widowers.
21. Ask young adults to help with holiday events which the church hosts to make contact with outsiders: trunk or treat, Thanksgiving Day meals, and Christmas gift giving.
22. Use young adults to help advertise coming special events by inviting their friends and even distributing information door-to-door.
23. Ask young adults to help with VBS by teaching or helping to put on skits that teach a specific lesson.

24. Use the young people to follow up on local visitors who have attended the services. Having a young person to make the call or the visit can be impressive to the visitor.
25. The young people can help with benevolence work—helping get the clothing and food room in good order or helping to distribute meals.

Holding on to and developing our young people is one of the most important things a church can do. Providing instruction, encouragement, training, and oversight of those of this age is critically important both to the present and to the future of the church. Give careful attention to it.

CHAPTER 13

THE MINISTRY FOR OLDER MEMBERS

Can be its Best

As people are now living longer, we naturally have more of the older generation in our congregations. Usually, these seniors will fall into two categories: those who need support and those who can serve. We will approach this chapter under those two headings.

Supporting the elderly

Certainly every congregation needs a plan for giving strong assistance to its elderly who live alone, who are home-bound, or who live in a care facility. Treating these members well achieves three beneficial outcomes. First, **we are obeying the Scriptures** as they tell us to be helpful. First Timothy 5:3 says, "Give proper recognition to those widows who are really in need" (NIV), and James 1:27 says we are to care for widows and orphans. Since many of our seniors are widows or widowers, we have instructions to care for them. And Galatians 6:2 instructs us to "Carry each other's burdens and in this way you will fulfill the law of Christ" (NIV).

The second beneficial outcome from supporting seniors is that **their needs will be met**. Many of them have grown old in our congregations, and we have loved them for many years. Certainly we want to fulfill their needs. Others have moved to our congregation recently, and we want to extend to them the beauty of Jesus that lives in us.

Still a third beneficial outcome from helping seniors is that **many**

HOW THE MINISTRY FOR OLDER MEMBERS *Can be its Best*

from outside our congregation will appreciate what we do for these older people. Their family members, their neighbors, and people in the community will note that we are caring for them in special ways, and this will cause them to think well of the church. What a great way to let our light shine! People will be drawn to a church that provides well for its older members. The following is a list of things to think about that can help a congregation do a great job in caring for older ones in need.

1. **Develop a special ministry to care for these older members.** Designate a deacon or someone else to provide good leadership as a ministry leader or committee chairman for this work. Larger congregations will likely have enough people in this category to need a part-time or full-time minister to lead in this work with seniors. The leader should also have helpers to keep the ministry running well. They can help him know who needs help and can divide the work. These leaders should recruit a group of people who will fill the needs of those who require help. Often, able-bodied older people can help to carry out this work.

2. **This ministry should make a list of all the older ones in the congregation who have needs the congregation can help meet.** Include those who live at home alone or with a care giver and those in a support facility. Also include all those who are widows or widowers even if they can take care of themselves because these often need opportunities for fellowship. Along with the name, address, phone number, birthday, and a family member to contact in case of a problem, note specific needs such as lawn care, house cleaning, meals, or transportation to church, to the doctor, and to shop. Also include a note about those who just need opportunities to be with others. The person's family should be helping with some of these needs if they are around, but the church should have a plan to help when it is needed.

3. **This ministry should have a specific plan for keeping in contact with all those on the list.** Some may need regular phone calls, cards, or visits. You need to know when a person needs assistance around the house or is sick and may need meals. This ministry will seek to know about each person's needs and have a plan to supply that need.

4. **The ministry must recruit and train a group of workers who devote themselves to assisting the elderly.**
   a. I know of a younger, single woman, for example, who has attached herself to an older woman needing help. She visits her regularly, has helped her learn how to use a walker, and takes her to church. This elderly woman and her husband know that their younger friend will be there for them whatever the need because she has maintained this relationship over many years.
   b. In many congregations, care for the elderly is primarily in the hands of retired people who are still are mobile, who need to be active in the Lord's work, so they render good service to those requiring assistance.
   c. Though announcements can be made about the need for laborers in this work, sometimes the leaders in this ministry may need to identify specific people they believe would be good helpers and make a direct request to them to join in this service.
5. **Here is a checklist of types of service the ministry should connect with those who need it.**
   a. Needs regular contact by phone, letter, email, or visits.
   b. Needs to be invited to meals, game nights, and other types of fellowship events.
   c. Needs help with tasks around the house such as lawn care, house cleaning, or meal preparation.
   d. Needs help with exercise, taking medicines, or other medical needs.
   e. Needs transportation to church, to shopping, to doctor appointments, and to fellowship events.
   f. Needs help in keeping in contact with family members.
6. **This ministry can also see that the seniors have good information on topics about aging on which they need excellent and easily understood information.** Having events to provide such information as the following can be publicized in the community to offer an opportunity for outreach.
   a. Navigating Social Security and Medicare.
   b. Financial planning for the retirement years.

HOW THE MINISTRY FOR OLDER MEMBERS *Can be its Best*

    c. Estate planning and how to make a will.

    d. Health issues during senior years.

    e. Making decisions about housing as the elderly go through various stages of life.

    f. Husbands and wives caring for mates during the aging process.

    g. Taking care of family members with dementia and related difficulties.

    h. Planning for the end of life about such matters as funerals, burial plans, and necessary notifications.

Using the elderly

In most congregations, there will be older people who are still quite active and who are a great source for carrying out good things that need to be done. This section begins with a list of ways in which such people can be used and then suggests a night each week in which many such activities can be carried out. The seniors ministry should provide to those in charge of various ministries in the church a list of older members who are still able to serve so they can locate ones who could help in their ministry.

1. Visit and make phone calls to the elderly, the sick, and those in the hospital and rest homes.
2. Visit those who have lost loved ones.
3. Grade correspondence courses that the congregation uses in prison work or such programs as World Bible School.
4. Make follow-up phone calls, write notes, and make visits those who have attended church services or special events or who have had children in programs such as VBS.
5. Help make contact with members who are missing services or who have been away for a while.
6. Assist with meal preparation, which the church provides for those who are having a funeral or for other special occasions.
7. Write letters or send emails to missionaries whom the congregation supports.
8. Care for the church lawn and flower beds.
9. Be greeters at the door for church services to welcome all, but especially to welcome visitors. These can also hand out bulletins and other information as people enter the building.

10. Take a section of the auditorium prior to the beginning of the Sunday services and walk around to greet people, particularly those who are visitors.
11. Help make a list of those who have stopped attending regularly and then assist with contacting them.
12. Help with children's Bible classes either to teach or to assist the teacher. Some children's classes, for example, need a person to assist with crafts, with helping children who are disturbing, or need to go to the rest room. They can assist in preparing handouts and crafts. They could also contact children who have missed class. Please don't think that elderly and the children of the church won't get along.
13. Help with the nursery during church services and Bible class.
14. Teach or assist with a home Bible study or one-on-one studies.
15. Connect with a local elementary or high school to assist a teacher, to mentor students needing assistance, or to be a sponsor when a group goes on a trip. Such services done in the name of the church certainly build goodwill for the congregation.
16. Volunteer at a hospital to greet visitors and help them find the person they wish to visit.
17. Host a booth for the church at a county fair or similar event. One church, for example, assists with serving watermelon at a city event. The city provides the watermelon and the church members, wearing their church ID badges, slice and serve.
18. Help plan worship and contact those who are to lead in various ways.
19. Assist with counting the contribution.
20. Assist with providing the communion on Sunday evening or taking communion to shut-ins.
21. Assist with maintaining the church directory.
22. Help with the church website.
23. Write articles about church events or people for the local newspaper.
24. Work with a local teenage group such as the FFA or connect with a high school sports team as chaplain (if allowed) or just as someone who hangs around with the team to know the players and help as the coach may request. One member did this so well and for so long that when the school built a new stadium, they named it after him.

25. Answer the phone at the church building or assist with things around the office such as copy work, mailing, and welcoming visitors to the building.
26. Serve at an information table in the lobby of the church building prior to services to greet visitors, give them information about the church, and help them find a class to attend.
27. Make CDs of sermons for those who request them.
28. Operate the sound booth for church services.
29. Provide a game night for seniors. This activity can provide fellowship opportunities for many who need it.
30. Be a discussion leader in a class for teens if the class is occasionally divided up for table talk.
31. Maintain the bulletin boards in the building with current informationand useful content. There can be bulletin boards with information about the different mission works the congregation supports and about various ministries of the church. One congregation has a long hallway between their auditorium and some of the classrooms where they have a display for each ministry of the church. Many smaller congregations have a board with pictures of the members. Put someone in charge to see that all members are represented, that new members are quickly photographed and posted, and that those no longer attending are taken down. Some congregations have a bulletin board with pictures of those who have passed on during the previous calendar year, which gives members a chance to remember and reflect.

One way in which many congregations involve both older and younger members is through what is often called Monday Night for the Master, a concept developed by Gary Bodine who currently preaches in Onalaska, Texas. On each Monday night (or another night of the week if preferred), the event begins at 6:00 p.m. with a simple meal for all who wish to come. Typically people are asked to contribute a small amount (like $3.00 or $4.00) to cover the cost of the meal. Those preparing, serving, and cleaning up after the meal are providing an important service. Everyone in the congregation is invited to come so that older people as well as younger ones, including families with children, can come to serve. The concept is that there will be work for all to do, and careful preparations have been made so assignments and materials will be ready. Babysitting is provided for those with smaller children, which offers a service opportunity to those who like to work with children.

Those who come to work have many services from which to choose: pray for others from a provided list; help with a study hall for children who come with their parents and need to study after doing a service; make visits to shut-ins, those in the hospital, those who have recently visited the congregation, and those who may have not attended recently; visit with people about starting a home Bible study; conduct a home Bible study; grade and mail correspondence courses; write thank-you cards to people in the congregation who render a service such a Bible school teachers, elders, deacons, ministers, and people who work behind the scenes; write to people who have recently visited; write to missionaries; and help teachers to prepare classroom materials. Other possibilities can be added in local situations such as calling people who have attended a previous VBS to inform them about an upcoming VBS; and calling, writing, or mailing information to invite people to attend upcoming special events.

For the aforementioned events that utilize a list with which to do such things as writing letters or cards or making visits, a worker has prepared the list in advance and has addresses, cards, paper, and pens ready for those who will need them.

On these Monday nights, there can also be training classes for those wanting to learn how best to visit those who have come to a service, how to reach out to those not attending, how to teach home studies, and how to lead in various elements of the worship service.

There are many benefits to such a program. Those who prepare for the activities, those who work with the meal, and those who direct each of the evening's activities have performed a special service, and many of these could be older people.

The work that gets done is important, and many of these things would be less likely to be accomplished without such a program. And a wide range of people from teens through seniors have important serving opportunities available to them. In fact, there are many people who would not be serving in such activities without this easy way to get involved.

THE MINISTRY FOR OLDER MEMBERS *Can be its Best*

Just show up. Eat a meal with others. Then choose to do something that is already planned and prepared to be done.

Additionally, there is great fellowship. For families coming with children, there is a good opportunity for intergenerational contact. On visits, for example, a teenager might be paired with a senior to visit someone at the hospital. And getting younger people involved in service at an early point in their lives is a great part of their spiritual development. Many who come for this activity may likely be widows and widowers who need opportunities to have contact with others. Eating a meal and being involved in serving together is a great uplift for them.

Think, too, of the benefits to the work of the congregation. With many more individuals serving to do so many things, consider the sheer number of tasks that would likely go undone if this program were not making it easy to accomplish them.

The Monday night for the Master program can be offered year round except for holiday weeks. It could also take a break for the summer if that seems wise. This plan is mentioned in this chapter for seniors, of course, because one of its greatest benefits is to offer seniors good ways to serve and to offer them an opportunity to spend time with others. The program, however, is a good thing for many besides the elderly.

Every congregation must consider what it needs to do to serve those who are older and how it can best use those who are older. Serve the elderly, and let the elderly serve.

CHAPTER 14

 THE BUILDINGS AND GROUNDS MINISTRY

Can be its Best

There is nothing in the New Testament about a congregation having its own building in which to meet. The church in Jerusalem met in the temple courts (Acts 2:46), and a group met in the home of Aquila and Priscilla (Acts 18:2-3). In Acts 20, Paul was preaching in the third floor of a house when Eutychus fell out of a window. No doubt they sometimes met in larger buildings or even outdoors. As the numbers grew, though, so did persecution, and large church gatherings were not safe in many places during the second and third centuries. In Rome, for example, Christians not only buried their dead in the catacombs, but met there, out of sight, to worship. As the persecution began to subside as the fourth century approached, however, church buildings began to be built. Interestingly some of the earliest known church facilities have been found in Egypt where the Roman persecution was not so evident.

As Christians no longer had to fear being discovered, they began to build church buildings, some of which were quite large. Ruins from a church building near Corinth, for example, are large enough that the church building likely would have accommodated about 2,000 people. The building had an adjoining baptistery and was built to focus attention toward the front of the assembly where, no doubt, stood the preacher and from which communion was served.

The requirement for Christians to meet weekly on Sunday is clear. Paul writes 1 Corinthians 12 and 14 about the public assembly. The letter to

HOW THE BUILDINGS AND GROUNDS MINISTRY *Can be its Best*

the Hebrews in 10:25 says Christians are not to forsake the assembly. The Scriptures also make clear what is to be done when Christians assemble: preach the Word, observe the Lord's Supper, pray, contribute, and sing.

With public assemblies required, there is an obvious implication that there must be an adequate place to meet.

The following are goals for keeping such facilities in good condition:

1. To make the auditorium as conducive to worship as possible with the audience able to hear and to keep themselves focused on those leading in the worship.
2. To have appealing classrooms, which are suitable for teaching and discussion.
3. To have the entire facility, both inside and out, to be attractive to the general public so as to be a credit to the community and to help the church to be well-respected.

Below are questions those overseeing the use of the building and grounds can check for ideas about things they might do to make the facility better at achieving its purpose.

Outside the building

1. Are the grounds around the building attractive with well-manicured lawns?
2. Are there well-kept flower beds and trees in appropriate places to make the facility attractive?
3. Are there attractive, large, and well-placed signs to identify the building clearly so people in the area will know about the facility and anyone else looking for the building can easily find it?
4. Is there attractive signage on main thoroughfares to help people to find the facility? (Signs that are not well-kept are a discredit to the church rather than an invitation to attend.)
5. Are all wooden parts of the outside of the building nicely painted in a suitable color?
6. Are there clearly marked parking spaces close to the main entrance, specifically for visitors?
7. Are there potholes in the parking lot?

8. Does the parking lot need to be upgraded from gravel to pavement or improved in some other way?
9. Do the lines that mark where cars should park need repainting?

In the lobby and hallways
1. Is the lobby area attractive and appealing to visitors?
2. Is there a desk or table in the lobby clearly marked for visitors with information they would find helpful?
3. Are there directional signs in the lobby that tell the visitor how to get to the auditorium, particular classrooms, and the fellowship hall?
4. Are restrooms clearly identified with signs not only on the doors, but signs directing people to them?
5. Are bulletin boards well-placed, up to date, and filled with pertinent information?
6. Are there stains on the carpet, the walls, or ceiling that would indicate that the building is not well-kept? (Such issues signal the visitor that this church does not do things well.)
7. Is everything well-swept and cleaned?

Now to the auditorium
1. Are the pews clean? Have they been polished recently?
2. Is the floor clean, well-swept, and free of debris?
3. Are the book racks clean and are songbooks well-distributed?
4. Are Bibles provided in the book racks?
5. Does the sound system work well? When a speaker addresses those in attendance, can people hear him when he first speaks? If not, is the problem either operator error or a low battery or is there another problem than could have been eliminated with careful attention? (It is a real distraction when there is a problem with the sound system. People get their minds out of a worshipful mode, and visitors conclude that you do not do things well at this church.)
6. Is the height of the pulpit such that a speaker, no matter his height, can be seen throughout the auditorium? Does the microphone placement block his face so that it is a distraction and keeps his facial expressions from being fully seen?

7. Does the background behind the speaker let him stand out without distraction? (Sometimes half of the speaker is in front of one background and the other half is in front of another—thus creating a distraction. Sometimes he has flowers "growing" out of his head. Sometimes the background is so much the color of his clothing that he fades out of sight. Sometimes the background is composed of rocks or drapes that draw attention away from the speaker.)

8. Is the baptistery in a position where all can see the person being immersed? Is there a microphone at the baptistery, which allows the person speaking to be heard throughout the building? Is the back of the baptistery painted so that the person being baptized can be seen well and in a way that people are not distracted by the background?

9. Does the lighting on the pulpit show the speaker well? (Probably need flood lights showing from both sides to light him equally on both sides. Eyes of the congregation will be drawn to where the brightest spot is, and that should be where the speaker is standing.)

10. Does the lighting of the area where the people sit provide enough brightness for them to be able to read their Bibles well during the sermon?

11. Is there a projector and screen, enabling the speaker and others to use PowerPoint? (Many congregations use PowerPoint on the screen as people are entering to provide announcements they need to know about. And many speakers now like to use PowerPoint in presenting their message.)

On to nursery, classrooms, and fellowship areas

1. Are the nursery facilities attractive and well-managed? (Many visitors who have small children look first at the nursery to see if they want to return.)

2. Do all the high school and adult classrooms have chairs of the appropriate size and are they all in good condition with no tears or defacing marks?

3. Are all the children's rooms furnished with appropriate tables and chairs for teachers and students? Are they all in good condition?

4. Are there marker boards and markers in all classrooms that could use them?
5. Does the fellowship room have tables and chairs, all in good condition with no marks or tears?
6. Are the walls in all the halls and rooms in good condition with no bad discoloration on ceiling, walls, or floors?
7. Is the kitchen, if there is one, provided with good equipment and adequate workspace? Does it need updating to provide the facilities for which people use it?

Now a few questions about the entire building

1. Does the air conditioning and heating equipment serve well and do the thermostats serve their function properly?
2. Is the roof in good condition or does it need some repairs?
3. Is the insurance adequate? Has the replacement value of the building gone up since the value indicated on the insurance was determined?
4. Is there a plan developed by an expert for how people would go to the safest place in case of a tornado? Do the proper leaders know of this plan and have people been informed?
5. Has a plan been made for how the people in the classrooms and in the auditorium will respond in case someone threatens those in the building? (Someone trained in the field should give advice and teachers and the elders and the preacher should learn what to tell the people to do.)
6. Should a uniformed officer be present during services to provide protection and to make it less likely that someone would attack? Some congregations now lock all but one door during the weekdays and have an officer at that unlocked door. (An expert in this type of situation could advise congregational leaders on the best thing to do.)

In some aspects of building care, those leading in the building and grounds area are doing their best job if no one notices much about the building and grounds. If the sound system is working perfectly, then no one thinks about the sound system. If the heating and cooling systems are doing their job regardless of outside temperatures, then people don't think about thanking someone, but if the temperature is not right, they will certainly want someone to know. If the building is always clean and well-kept, people don't notice, but if it isn't, then many will notice. The point is that this is a vital area of work which, but one many will think about if all goes well. Those in this area must take satisfaction if no one says anything to them. Hopefully, there will be leaders who will say thanks when all goes well.

CHAPTER 15

THE WORSHIP MINISTRY

Can be its Best

God's people have always been called to worship Him. Their worship is first for His glory and then for their own spiritual growth. The Israelites were to remember the Sabbath Day because that was their special day to think about God. Christians are told not to forsake the assembly (Hebrews 10:25) because God knows we need to be regular in our worship to Him and to be with one another.

A good way to teach people about the purposes of worship is to use four different verses from the New Testament.

1. Our worship is to "proclaim the Lord's death until He comes" (1 Corinthians 11:26, NIV), so we worship *to proclaim* God and our faith in Him. We want everyone to know about our God.

2. Our worship is also to "offer...a sacrifice of praise" to God, Christ, and the Holy Spirit (Hebrews 13:15, NIV). This means that in every different act of worship such as singing, praying, taking communion, engaging in the sermon, or giving, we should be seeking to *adore* Him.

3. Worship also involves engaging God, Christ, and the Holy Spirit in communication: "singing and making melody to the Lord with your heart" (Ephesians 5:19, ESV). We send messages to God to thank Him, send our messages of repentance, and making our requests. And, on the other hand, as we read the Bible and listen to a message

from His Word, He speaks to us. So, as we speak to Him and He speaks to us, in our worship we seek *to communicate*.

4. Our worship is a time to *edify* or build up one another (1 Corinthians 14:26). God designed our worship to Him both to be for honoring Him and, at the same time, for strengthening one another. Think of these four words: *proclaim, adore, communicate,* and *edify*. As we are achieving our main purpose in worship to praise and glorify God, we also are having an opportunity to proclaim Him and communicate with Him, and while we are doing this, God reciprocates by making that very act a way of strengthening us. For Christians to be together in worship has, then, both as vertical and a horizontal aspect, but we must place the vertical one first.

So, teach the congregation about *proclaim, adore, communicate,* and *edify*. To help them remember these words, tell them that the first letters in the four words together spell "PACE." Tell of these four words in a bulletin article and in posters around the building and on the projection screen. Ingrain in the minds of your congregation the purposes for worship, so they will think of these as they participate in the worship occasion.

Many New Testament passages report on what Christians did when they came together. Acts 20:6 says Paul waited seven days to meet with the church at Troas, so he could be there on the first day of the week to participate with them in "breaking bread," an expression referring to taking the Lord's Supper. And on that occasion he preached to them until midnight (v. 7). In 1 Corinthians 16:1-2 Paul tells the Corinthian church to take up a collection at their first day of the week meetings. In 1 Corinthians 14, Paul gives lengthy instructions about the collective worship, speaking about singing, praying, and instructing in their assemblies.

So Christians are to meet each first day of the week to proclaim, adore, communicate, and edify. Our all-wise Father, made our worship to Him likewise to be beneficial to us. An old story tells of an elder who, on a cold winter night, went to see a member of his church who was not attending regularly. Asked to come in and sit by the fireplace, the elder said nothing, but after a few minutes just took the tongs by the fire and set one small piece of glowing wood off to itself. Soon its glow was gone, and it died.

Still without a word, the elder got up and left. He had made his point, and the wayward member was at church the next Sunday.

Conducting a worship service that is scriptural in what it does, in the way it should be done, and to achieve the God-given purposes for which it is done lies at the heart of the church. So, here are some suggestions to consider about strengthening various elements of worship. By studying this list of ways a congregation might improve its worship, you will likely find some things you would like to try. Making our worship the best it can be should be the aim of every congregation.

Communion

In 1 Corinthians 11, Paul addresses ways in which the Corinthian church was not properly observing the Lord's Supper and, to emphasize their failure to keep this part of worship as he had instructed them, he said they were eating and drinking judgment on themselves. That's a powerful statement about the importance of properly remembering the meaning of the bread and cup as we take them. Here are some suggestions that can help members take the communion in the most meaningful way.

1. Before taking communion, sing a song about Jesus' death and resurrection. Occasionally read the words of the song before singing it to focus minds on the meaning of the supper as expressed in the song.

2. Before taking the Lord's supper, read a passage from Matthew 26:26-30, Mark 14:22-26, or Luke 22:14-35, which tell how Jesus instituted this worship event. Or use some other appropriate passage. The two central elements of the meaning of the communion may be summarized by the words *sacrifice* and *atonement*. These words can show on the screen in the shape of a cross with "atonement" vertical and "sacrifice" horizontal. Jesus went through the most terrible experience of physical pain but, even worse, was the mental anguish. No one has ever suffered as He did while, during it all, having the power to stop it any time He wished. Remember, He could have called 10,000 angels. And this great "sacrifice" was for our "atonement" as He paid the price for our sins.

3. Read from 1 Corinthians 11:17-34 and explain that the Corinthian Christians were not taking the Lord's Supper properly and how we must give this the greatest attention.

4. Before taking the Lord's Supper, someone can make comments reminding people of the meaning and perhaps incorporating one of the above passages or other related ones. He may also remind people of all those around the world with whom they are sharing this event on that day and of all the millions since the first century with whom they are sharing communion.
5. Be sure that those leading in prayers or making comments speak loudly enough. Even with a microphone, the men must speak up. It does not help people get in the mind to take the supper if they cannot hear what is said.
6. Passing the Lord's Supper is a good time to begin to work younger men into leading the worship, so let teenagers be among those who pass the elements and say the prayers.
7. Do not rush this part of the service. Give proper time for members quietly to reflect on Jesus' sacrifice for us and how we should be responding to that. Are they repenting, are they re-committing, are they resolving?

Song Service

Singing was clearly a significant part of the worship of the early church. In Ephesians 5:19, Paul tells Christians to sing to one another using psalms, hymns, and spiritual songs, making melody in their hearts to the Lord. So, we sing to one another, and we sing to the Lord. Here are some suggestions about the singing in our worship.

1. Connect songs before and after the sermon to the theme the preacher is using and sing about Jesus' death and resurrection before the communion. To do this, songs will need to be chosen in advance of the service.
2. Vary the speed at which songs are sung. Some songs are most meaningful when sung slowly and quietly, while others are best sung more rapidly and more loudly. Sometimes the speed can even change from verse to verse in the same song. The song leader should choose the proper speed to help people sense the meaning more clearly.
3. Use different volumes in singing songs. Some praise songs, for

example, call for full volume, while some meditative songs should be sung softly.

4. Occasionally read the words of a song before it is sung to give emphasis to the meaning of the words. Or just a sentence before the song like "Let's join our hearts in this hymn of praise to God" can remind people to think about the words more clearly.

5. The congregation should be taught to recognize to whom the song is directed. In some songs we sing to teach and encourage one another. In other songs we direct our thoughts to God to honor and praise Him. In still other cases, the words are God's as He is speaking to us. The words may even be directed to those outside the church to encourage them to come to Jesus. Occasionally the one to whom the song is directed even changes from verse to verse. So a great way to help people think about the meaning of a song is to teach them to think about whether they are speaking to one another, or to God, or to outsiders, or that God is speaking to them. As examples, note that in "O For a Faith That Will Not Shrink," we sing the first three verses to encourage each other while the fourth verse is a prayer to God. In "I Gave My Life for Thee," Jesus speaks to us through all four verses. In "Jesus Paid It All," Jesus speaks to us in the first verse, we speak to Him in the second verse, and in the third verse we state our commitment. The chorus after each verse of this song is a declaration we are making to others. Since the congregation needs to be aware of such shifts to be able to sing such songs well, we need to teach how they should be alert to recognize whether we are speaking to God, He is speaking to us, or we are speaking to others.

6. Sometimes the song leader can say a sentence or two prior to singing a song to emphasize its meaning. For example, prior to singing "When We All Get to Heaven," he might say, "We are about to sing to one another that we all want to be in heaven together. Keep this in mind as we sing." Or prior to singing "All Hail the Power of Jesus' Name," he might say, "We are about to call on people everywhere and even on angels to glorify the name of Jesus. Let's mean this sincerely." Prior to singing "How Great Thou Art," the leader could remind the

audience that "We are singing this song to God. Think that you are standing before His throne and singing directly to Him."

7. Since we are to sing "one to another," the leader might occasionally have all to stand and ask those on the left and right sides of the auditorium to face each other. Then they could sing alternative verses of a song like "If the skies above you are gray," with one side singing the first and third verses and the other side singing verse two and then all singing to each other the chorus. That would emphasize the fact that we sometimes "sing one to another in psalms, hymns, and spiritual songs."

8. Have a Wednesday night class for a quarter in which you primarily sing songs. You can work some on the musical aspects of a song, but primarily the teacher can emphasize the meaning of a song you are about to sing. He can read Scriptures and make comments appropriate to the song, and then all can sing the song meaningfully together. Such a class is a good time to learn some new songs that could later be used in a worship service because many will have learned the song in the Wednesday night class. One congregation has such a class every summer. They call the class "WOW," which stands for Wonder of Worship.

9. There are various approaches about the use of older and newer songs. Some want to sing many newer songs to appeal primarily to those who are young. Other congregations sing only the older, familiar songs because they have done that for years. A number of factors must be considered in working to find the right balance. Here are a few suggestions.

    a. If a congregation has sung only older hymns for many years, introduce two or three new songs slowly and only those that are easy to sing.

    b. Be sure that some in the congregation know the new song before singing it in the worship, so it will not be only the leader singing.

    c. In introducing a newer song, be sure that it fits the sermon or communion exceptionally well, which will make the congregation more accepting.

    d. Even if the congregation has learned many new songs, keep the balance so those who still prefer the older songs are not left out and those who like the newer ones have a chance to sing them.

e. Consider the visitors who are coming and what type of songs they would most likely know. You want them to feel included. If, for example, they are likely only to know older ones and you sing only newer ones, they won't be able to participate well and will feel uncomfortable.

f. Be sure the audience knows the first two or three songs in a service, so they get the feeling that they can participate well in the singing. That means not to sing new songs at the very beginning of the service.

10. Occasionally, maybe the fourth Wednesday night of each month through the summer, have a song service in which young people lead—from high school age down even to pre-schoolers. We need to train our youth to lead, and we need to give them a sense of involvement. Such a service can also provide some good intergenerational experiences as the older members tell the younger members that they did well. And this service can give an opportunity to teach how one should give careful attention to the words of songs.

11. The song leader should know well the songs he plans to lead so he can look at the audience most of the time when they are singing.

12. If the church has a projection system, it is good to project the words and music of the song on the screen. This gets the people looking up instead of down and their voices can be more easily heard. The number in the hymnal for each of the songs should be included on the first two or three slides so those preferring a book may use it, but projecting the words and the music on songs speeds up the service by removing the time for looking up the songs in the book.

13. Some suggest that a congregation develop a collection of about 50 songs, which they can come to know well and from which the song leaders choose their hymns for each service. With 50 songs in a collection and with five or so songs used each service, a song would be repeated only every 10 services or about every month and a half. Occasionally, of course, additional songs could be added to the collection.

Prayer

In 1 Corinthians 14:15, Paul is discussing the Corinthian worship assembly, and he says that they should pray with the spirit, but also with understanding. He also mentions others saying "Amen" when a person gives thanks. Acts 4:23-31 tells of a prayer meeting about Peter and John being in prison, and the congregation prayed for their release. In prayer we express praise, give thanks, appeal for blessings on the kingdom, and make requests. Below are some thoughts about how to make the prayers in our assemblies more meaningful.

1. Teach the congregation to make the words of the person leading the prayer to be their words. One person "leads" the prayer, but we should all be praying together.
2. Have a session with the men and boys who might lead a prayer to teach them about such things as:
    a. The purpose of prayer by studying several passages about prayer, particularly 1 John 5:14, Ephesians 5:18, and Matthew 6:9-13.
    b. When we pray, we are entering the throne room of God, so prayer should be thought of as a solemn experience and a great honor.
    c. Prayers should be an appropriate length with the prayers for the bread and cup being fairly short, the closing prayer being longer, and a prayer earlier in the service being up to three or four minutes long.
    d. The primary prayer in the service should start with some statements of praise and thanks for God's blessings. Then there should be requests about some aspects of the work of the church such as missionaries, local ministers, some of the current efforts of the church, requests about individual members of the church who have special needs, and then a close in the Jesus name.
    e. Prayers for the Lord's Supper should include references to such topics as Jesus' being willing to come to earth as a man, to the sacrifice He made in being crucified, and to His resurrection from the dead to become the head of the church.
    f. The prayer for the contribution should ask the Lord's blessing on the use of the funds to spread the gospel message and to bless the poor, and the prayer could ask God to help those making decisions about the use of the money.

g. Prayers should be specific by mentioning missionaries by name and not just in general. Those who are sick should be mentioned specifically not just by "all the sick."

h. Those leading in prayer should speak loudly and should speak directly into the microphone if there is one. The audience can't participate with them unless they can understand them.

i. Those leading in prayer should think in advance about those who need to be included in the prayer, about some of the ministries they want especially to mention, and about how they want to express praise and appreciation.

3. Those planning the worship should fairly often include a prayer in addition to those typically given that only mention one topic. This special prayer might be given for a family who has lost a loved one; for the youth of the congregation to be faithful; for the ministers of the church; for a particular ministry in the church; for the elderly; for widows and widowers; for a member who is critically ill; for the rulers of the city, state, or nation; for the blessing of living in a land of religious freedom; for one being baptized; for parents; for a Christian school; for the local schools; for local police and firemen; for those affected by a disaster; or other matters that especially need God's blessing.

Contribution

1. Read a New Testament passage about the contribution such as 1 Corinthians 16:1, appropriate verses from 2 Corinthians 8 and 9, or Acts 2:45.

2. Before the contribution, share some specifics about something the contribution will support such as a foreign missionary, something about the education program or a VBS, or some other good work.

3. Put information in the bulletin about good works the contribution supports. Remember, you must tell people numerous times about how their money will be spent and how their gifts will benefit others.

4. Be open with the congregation about the budget, the amounts of the contribution, and how the money is used. Answer any questions anyone has about the contribution.

HOW THE WORSHIP MINISTRY *Can be its Best*

Sunday Night Service

In most congregations, the Sunday night service sees fewer people in attendance than in previous years. Some use small groups on Sunday night and believe the closer contact with other members is beneficial. Most congregations, however, continue with the service on Sunday night believing that hearing another sermon grounded in Scripture and being together as a congregation has important benefits. For those who continue to have the evening service, here are some thoughts about how to make that service useful, inspiring, and interesting to more people. If your church decides to implement any of these ideas, advertise the events in the bulletin, maybe in a special mailing, by announcement in the Sunday morning services, and even in Bible classes.

1. Once a year, host a service in which parents can bring their babies born in the preceding year so elders and others may pray about the parents bringing up their child in the nurture and admonition of the Lord. The lesson of the evening should be about the importance of parenting and provide some suggestions for parents.

2. Elementary and high school boys who are capable should regularly be asked to offer prayers and Scripture readings. Once or twice a year, the young men should conduct the entire service. This will be good for their spiritual growth and contact with the church, and their involvement will attract their parents and others to come to support them.

3. Pair high school students on one Sunday night a month for three months with an older couple. They should sit with them at church and to go together with them for a meal before or after the service. We need to do more intergenerational things, and this would be a helpful experience.

4. Occasionally have a family night on Sunday night when all the members of a family sit together. Emphasize the lesson on family matters.

5. Different adult classes could conduct a devotion for 15 minutes prior to the sermon and would encourage all the members of that class to come.

6. If the congregation is participating in Leadership Training for Christ, Lads to Leaders, or some similar program for youth, let the young men use what they are learning to do—lead a song, read a Scripture, make a short talk, sing as a group—as part of the evening service. This will give them a chance to show the congregation what they are learning and will enhance their experience with the program for youth. It will also encourage the parents who have children involved in the program to attend.

7. If missionaries are visiting, let them speak at the evening service, and advertise it well to the congregation.

8. Choose special topics for the study on Sunday night: sexual questions, abortion, gambling, salvation by faith alone, etc. A congregation could even have a Bible question-and-answer session with the preacher and elders answering the questions. This would be a good topic to be advertised so those not usually attending on Sunday night would want to come.

9. Conduct a special prayer time for missionaries, some in the congregation who are ill or have lost loved ones, for the youth, for the nation, or other matters of special interest.

10. Have a service anchored in the Bible, but which fits the time of year—New Year's Day, Christmas, Thanksgiving, Easter. Outsiders who do not regularly attend church are more likely to come to such occasions than they are to attend a typical service. Ask your members to invite friends.

11. Invite special speakers who could speak on Sunday morning and on Sunday night. Advertise these both in the congregation and in the community.

12. On the Sunday nearest to Valentine's Day, have a special service celebrating marriages. Identify those in your congregation who have celebrated 50 or more years together, and honor them especially.

General Observations

1. Think carefully about how you begin each worship service. You should, of course, welcome visitors warmly. Following that, however, a long string of announcements does not make an inviting start. Try to cover the information the congregation needs in a handout, in your weekly

bulletin, or even on the screen before the service. If there are things which merit special mention, put those comments just before the end of the service. This might be the announcement of a death and funeral or a serious illness that needs special attention or it might be encouragement for people to visit someone in the hospital or to attend some special event.

By getting quickly into the songs and prayers, those attending are more likely to get into the spirit of worship than if they sit through 8-10 minutes of announcements. A visitor, to whom these announcements have no meaning, will be particularly disappointed by such a beginning to the service.

2. Some congregations whose buildings allow for adjustments to the level of the lights like to change them for various aspects of worship. They put the auditorium lights, for example, at a lower level during communion, while the speaker and others involved at the front are lighted by a different system. This may help establish a thoughtful mood, but since many like to read appropriate passages from their Bibles during the communion, the lighting level should not be too dim.
3. Lighting on the pulpit area should certainly be bright during the sermon. Some buildings do not have enough special lighting such as flood lights on the pulpit area and that fails to use the lighting to draw attention to the speaker. To keep the focus on those leading the service, make every effort to illuminate them.
4. Give considerable thought to the background behind those speaking from the pulpit. A smooth, lighter-colored surface is the best—either painted or with a plain, light-colored curtain. A background of bricks, stones, or similar surfaces can distract because people may be drawn to put their attention on the background rather than on the speaker.
5. A worship service should be carefully planned and not be something put together at the last minute. The songs should be carefully chosen in advance to fit together and to harmonize with the lesson and other elements of the service. The invitation song should match the final appeal of the sermon. Choose and contact in advance those who are to lead various elements of the service so they can give some thought to their part of the service.

Bringing the Christian community together to praise and honor God, to beseech Him in prayer, to hear a message from Him through His Word, and to offer contributions to show our love for Him is so important. God asks us to do it and gives us directions on how to do it. God's wisdom is shown in the worship because what He tells us to do to honor Him is also beneficial to our spiritual lives. The worship of false gods is often destructive by being immoral, by being physically harmful, and by being mentally damaging. God, however, designed our worship to Him both to honor Him and to be beneficial to us.

Our gathering to worship God, then, should be carefully planned, designed to help each person present to focus on entering God's presence with proper thoughts. It is a time of deep thought and even of strong emotion as we present ourselves before God's throne with a message in our hearts for Him.

CHAPTER 16

 A CHURCH'S WEBSITE
Can be its Best

The story in the Book of Acts makes it abundantly clear that members of the church did things to make both the church and individual Christians to be well-known. Even the Holy Spirit did this on the Day of Pentecost because He chose to come on the apostles when they were where a large crowd could see the tongues of fire and hear the wind and the apostles speaking in languages. Why did the Holy Spirit come in such a place and in such a way? It was to set the stage for Peter to preach to thousands, 3,000 of whom were baptized on that day.

Acts 2 continues to tell about these early Christians by describing how some sold their goods to share with those in need. And "every day they continued to meet together in the temple courts" (v. 45, NIV). As a result of this they enjoyed "the favor of all the people" (v. 47, NIV).

Acts 3 tells that Peter and John healed a lame man who was publicly known because he had sat at the gate to the temple every day. When the crowd there saw him walking and leaping, they were drawn together to hear Peter preach again.

Acts 4 tells that Peter and John continued to preach in the temple courts and "many who heard the message believed, and the number of the men grew to about five thousand" (v. 4, NIV). When Peter and John were called before the rulers and elders, they wanted to shut them up, but realized "Everyone living in Jerusalem knows they have performed a notable sign" (v. 16, NIV).

HCW A CHURCH'S WEBSITE *Can be its Best*

Through the miracles the Lord empowered the apostles to do and through their good living, people quickly learned about the church. Though we still have good living to let people know about us, we don't have the miracles anymore. **And every church needs to make itself known through having a well-designed, up-to-date website.** That is where many will go to see what they can learn about your congregation. If your website is well-done, has good information, and is easy-to-use, then your congregation gets a positive reaction, which may lead someone to attend or to check the church out in other ways. A poorly done website, however, will certainly hinder further contact. Be sure you have a great website because that will help you both share information and make a good impression.

The information below will first give a checklist of ideas about the things that you must have available on your website and will follow that with a few ideas about how to get started if you do not yet have a website.

Basic to any analysis of your website, you must consider who will be going to your website and what they will be seeking. In the following listing, we will look at how your website should serve different categories of people, and there will be some repetition of items as we view these groups.

1. **Serving members of your congregation**
   A. Members will be looking to **find such information as**:
      1. The time and place of special events such as seminars and guest speakers and the benefits of attending.
      2. Regular service times, especially if you have some variation over the summer or during holiday periods.
      3. A copy of your weekly bulletin that a member may have missed if you distribute it on Sundays.
      4. Information on how to contact elders, staff members, and directors of various ministries.
      5. Information on how to get involved or to learn more about various ministries.
   B. Members will be going to the website to **take the following actions**, so set up your website to serve these purposes:

1. To sign up for events.
2. To listen to sermons they have missed or want to hear again.
3. To download materials for teaching or handouts for students in a Bible class.
4. To contact elders and staff members.
5. To make contributions online, which allows those who wish to have a regular withdrawal from their bank account.
6. To access social media sites.
7. To find assignments they are to carry out about visiting and serving in other ways.
8. To access your member information system for addresses, phone numbers, and other secure data if you have connected with a service company to supply such information. These items typically are put on a server besides your own system for which you pay a maintenance fee. See more information below.

2. **Serving non-members of your congregation**
    A. Non-members will be looking to **find such information as**:
       1. A brief statement about your fundamental beliefs and your approach to Scripture. You could look online to review several statements to get some ideas and styles. Be sure to make the statement clear, but not confrontational.
       2. Identity of the staff members and leaders. This is usually placed under the heading of "About Us" and should have a name, position, picture, and contact information, including the email address and phone numbers.
       3. The address, specific directions, and a picture of the church building. Some have instructions on how to get there or a map on which the location is noted.
       4. The times of Sunday and Wednesday services and classes. If you have variations such as a Sunday afternoon service and no evening service on the first Sunday of each month, be sure to note those times, so a visitor does not come and find no one at the building. You could also note such things as week-day morning classes for women or a men's breakfast.

5. Any meals you regularly provide for visitors. If, for example, you serve lunch to visitors each Sunday after morning service, have lunch once a month after service, or provide something else special for visitors, be sure to list these.
6. Special events approaching. The non-member might be interested in an upcoming marriage or parenting seminar so put in a little bit of "sell" about it. (This will be good for members who go to the site as well.)
7. Your provisions for children. This is one of the points of most interest for possible visitors who have children. Describe your nursery and tell how it is protected and tell about childcare during services. Of course, be sure to tell about the Bible classes for children on Sunday morning and Wednesday nights. Also include information about all your programs for teens.
8. Information about various ministries you have. You don't have to give long explanations for each, but you could, for example, list under "missions" the different countries where you support missionaries and under "benevolence" any programs you offer for those with special needs. People checking out whether they want to become associated with your church would like to know what you do and where they might fit in.
9. A statement about "next steps." List the person one might contact for more information and how to contact that person. If you have a class for those just connecting with your church, you could note something about that.

B. Non-members will want to go to the website to take the following actions, so set up your website to handle these items:
1. Contact someone with questions.
2. Sign up for events.
3. Listen to sermons of the local preacher or a recent guest speaker.
4. Get directions to the building.

3. **Serving visitors from out-of-town**
   A. Visitors from out-of-town will be looking to find the following information:

1. Times for Sunday and Wednesday services.
   2. Information on special events.
   3. Contact information for elders and staff.
   B. Actions they may want to take:
      1. Get information on whom to call to get help in case of an accident or because they are stranded. A note about such occasions on your website would send the message to all who go there that you are a caring congregation.
      2. Get directions to the building.

4. **Serving people of your community**
   A. People of your community not looking for a church, but who might want to find information about the congregation might want to know about:
      1. Special events you are hosting.
      2. Times of services.
      3. Contact information about elders or staff or ministry directors.
   B. People of your community might want to take the following actions:
      1. Sign up for special events.
      2. Call to get help.
      3. Contact someone to answer questions.
      4. Get directions to the building.

Having seen who will be the possible users of your website and what they will be seeking, the following are some general suggestions for your website.

   1. **Make sure the website visually looks like your congregation**. Do the style of the fonts, the pictures, and the colors reflect the nature of your congregation? Are you in a rural area or a city? Are you more formal or less formal? Do you want to give the appearance of younger or older? Look at the site through the lens of those you think will be using the website and see it through their eyes. Can people to whom you are appealing see people like themselves in your pictures?

2. **Be sure the website is easy to use.** Have good headings that direct people to specific information with easy-to-read type that can help them get where they want to go.
3. **Be sure the content is current.** Information changes often—different people, different events, different times. Be sure everything is up-to-date. Those who are interested in finding out more about you will interpret out-of-date information as a strike against you.
4. If there is a list of churches for your city, be sure your website is listed on it since people often start there in looking for a church. If your Chamber of Commerce has a list of churches for new people coming to town, find out how to get on it and get your website listed.
5. Be sure your website shows up on search engines like Google and Bing, so people searching the internet for churches in your area will easily find your listing.

The headings which often appear on church websites are listed below with a note about what is under each heading.

- **About**—Beliefs, Elders, Deacons, Staff, Location. Each person listed can be shown with contact information and a picture.
- **Ministries**—a listing of each ministry in the congregation such as Bible classes, missions, benevolence, youth, local outreach, building and grounds, women's programs, men's programs, and others. With each may be a picture showing people at work in that ministry and a link to find out who to contact if a person is interested in doing that work or in finding out more about it.
- **Media**—recent bulletins, audios, or videos of sermon.
- **Contact**—a way to email someone at the church with a question or statement.
- **Give**—a way to contribute if a member would like to have the weekly contribution or a special amount taken from his/her bank account.
- **Online Community**—connecting to the members and other secure information that may be reached only through having a password so that such information about members is not open to the public.

If you don't have a website or want to get a new start with one, here are some things you could do.

1. **Find someone to help.** You might locate someone in your congregation who has website skills who's willing to volunteer their time. They might be able to provide good advice or may have the skills to do the work themselves. You might also engage a professional to help. If you do, be sure to check their references, see some sites they have built, and be clear with them about the total budget and time frame for building your site. Whomever you find to help can assist you with the rest of the steps below.

2. **Register your domain name.** The domain name is your unique address on the internet. Most churches use a domain name that ends in *.org*, which indicates they are a nonprofit organization. Each domain name is unique, so you will have to select one that no one else is already using. There is process and fee you will pay to register your domain name with a domain name registrar. This is not difficult and often the place that hosts your site can assist in this process.

3. **Find a place to host your site.** Websites are hosted (stored) on a computer that is permanently connected to the internet. A wide range of companies offer to rent you a place to host your website. Most of these will have a monthly or annual charge for this service.

4. **Plan and build your website.** Just like you plan a building before it is constructed, you should take the time to plan out the content, function, and organization of your website. Use the ideas in this chapter and ideas you might get from looking at other churches' websites. You will want to make sure that whoever is building your website is using tools that will allow you to make changes to the information on the website after they are done. You should expect them to get it started, but you will want someone on the church staff to be able to make frequent updates. Once it is built, your site can be set up on the location you have identified to host your site.

5. **Keep your website up to date.** Each week you will want to update anything that has changed and post any new information (new events, most recent bulletin, new members, etc.), and you will want to remove outdated information about events and people who have left. Visitors to your site will know immediately whether your site is regularly maintained.

HOW A CHURCH'S WEBSITE *Can be its Best*

Your website, even more than signs you place along the road or in front of your building, is now a vital means not only for sharing information, but also for sharing who you are. Be sure your website not only has good information, but also has a good appearance and is easy-to-use.

CHAPTER 17

THE FELLOWSHIP AT CHURCH
Can be its Best

The word *fellowship* is used in a variety of ways in the New Testament such as fellowship with God and fellowship with darkness. In this chapter, however, we are speaking of the fellowship Christians have with one another through being together in worship and through the association they have with one another in various ways.

The first mention of this "fellowship" in the church comes in Acts 2:42, just after the church begins on Pentecost. That passage says "they devoted themselves to the apostles' teaching and to fellowship, to the breaking of bread and to prayer." The term here may have something to do with fellowship in worship since it is listed with teaching, the Lord's Supper, and prayers. The next few verses, however, go on to mention their eating in one another's homes and telling about those who sold possessions to help those who had needs. From then on, such fellowship in the church is mentioned often either by describing fellowship that is happening or by encouraging Christians to be involved in fellowship with other saints.

Often, fellowship in the church is found in worshiping together: "And let us consider how to stir up one another to love and good works, not neglecting to meet together" (Hebrews 10:25, ESV). One outcome of meeting with the brethren regularly for worship is that we stir up each other to love and good works. When we gather for worship we come to praise God and we come to strengthen one another. The very act of worshiping together, then, provides strong fellowship that helps us grow in the Lord.

HOW THE FELLOWSHIP AT CHURCH *Can be its Best*

In Philippians 2:2, Paul calls Christians to a second type of fellowship. "Make my joy complete by being like-minded, having the same love, being one in spirit and of one mind" (NIV). Doing those things that show we love one another and enjoying a sense of unity is another aspect of fellowship. Some churches, unfortunately, have factions and are split over issues that are not essential matters of faith. They have unresolved differences over what to do with their money, with who should be leading in various works of the church, over the types of songs to sing, over how to do their benevolence work, over whether to plant a new church. These are not unimportant matters, but they are less important than the unity of the church. Being of the same mind is essential to good fellowship.

Three other passages add to our understanding of fellowship:

- 1 Thessalonians 5:11 says to "encourage one another to build one another up" (ESV).
- Hebrews 10:24 says to "stir up one another to love and good works" (ESV).
- Galatians 6:2 adds that we are to "bear one another's burdens, and so fulfill the law of Christ" (ESV).

With these passages in mind, here are some suggestions about building up fellowship among Christians in your congregation. Some of these suggestions will involve possibilities for the whole church, and some will deal with how smaller groups and individuals can promote fellowship. Even if something just puts six or eight members together, that can provide important fellowship for those involved. Have enough different small occasions to be able to touch all the members.

1. **To encourage fellowship when the church is assembled:**
   a. Have greeters at the door to welcome both guests and members. Make all feel warmly welcome.
   b. Have greeters who work each section of the auditorium before the service, just shaking hands and having conversations. Sometimes people ask the greeter a question about the church or make some comment they have on their minds. This contact is not difficult, yet it can increase the sense of fellowship.

c. Encourage all members to greet those on the row where they are sitting and those in front or behind them. Some who sit together each Sunday really take advantage of the time before and after the worship to catch up with close friends.
d. Teach the church to recognize that all are together in worship—they are in a common effort to praise God and to learn from His Word. As members sense that all are in union offering praise to God, they increase their sense of fellowship with everyone else.
e. Teach the church that as they take the communion, they have a common bond as they all are showing appreciation for what Jesus has done for us. Beyond that, they are sharing in this bread and fruit of the vine with people all over the world, and even beyond that, they are sharing in this "meal" with Christians who have lived all the way back to the apostles and to Jesus. "What a fellowship, what a joy divine."
f. Occasionally during worship, sing a song of encouragement and have the two sides of the congregation stand and face each other as they sing it. "Addressing one another in...spiritual songs" (Ephesians 5:19, ESV).
g. Teach that since this common worship experience is a time for us to strengthen and encourage one another, so members should linger a while after the service to visit.
h. Occasionally have lunch after church to give members a time for fellowship, thus building stronger ties among members. Find ways to get those less attached to attend these occasions such as having someone give them a special invitation. Also use the bulletin and public announcements to encourage all to attend.

2. **Use Bible classes as a time of fellowship:**
    a. Encourage all to be in a class. Determine which members regularly do not attend a class and have a class member of an appropriate class invite them come to their class. Some of the best fellowship can happen within class groups.
    b. Allow a few minutes before class for people to mingle, providing

HOW THE FELLOWSHIP AT CHURCH *Can be its Best*

time for people to know one another better and to welcome visitors and those new to class.

   c. Have lots of opportunities for fellowship through which those attending the same Bible class can strengthen ties with one another: meals together after the Sunday night service, short trips together in a church van or bus on a Sunday morning to visit and strengthen a smaller church in the area, going together in a vehicle to some special restaurant a few miles away for a meal together, and going together to some sports event.

3. Encourage members to do things together such as having a workday at the church or helping a widow at her home, having a booth at the county fair, helping at an inner-city church, serving together at a local public event, or cleaning up a section of a highway. Working together is a great way to develop stronger relationships with one another.

4. A group can do door-to-door work to advertise some special event at the church.

5. Work up a group that goes to rest homes or even to the homes of shut-ins to sing for people.

6. Have an hour of singing hymns at a members' home to which class members are encouraged to attend.

7. Have a regularly scheduled men's breakfast to bring together some of the men for fellowship.

8. Arrange a regularly scheduled ladies' luncheon, maybe after the ladies Bible class, so the women can have a good opportunity for fellowship.

9. Some ladies like to quilt or make baby blankets to take to newborns. Such opportunities bring members together for fellowship as well as for the good they do.

10. Have a phone team which divides up those members who are home-bound either permanently or temporarily to give calls of encouragement.

11. Gather another team to send cards to those who have been baptized, are ill, have lost a loved one, or who are homebound. If they can do

this together in the same room as they do their work, they will find good fellowship.

12. Have a team that meets monthly to send notes of thanks to various people who do work in the church—elders, preachers, Bible school teachers, those who prepare the communion, who care for the building, those who contact missionaries, or those doing any other work at the church. Those thanked will feel closer to the congregation and so will those who do the thanking.

13. Develop prayer teams who meet regularly to pray for those in the church with special needs, to pray for the work of the church, to pray about special events and efforts coming up, and to pray for the community and for the nation. Those who pray together will be joined in fellowship, and God will hear and respond to their prayers.

14. Members who live in smaller communities may want to make a trip together to a larger city where they can shop together or attend together a concert or a sporting event. Talking in the vehicle together and doing something together builds relationships.

15. Create small group Bible studies, and encourage as many of the members to participate as possible. Someone can suggest Bible passages to study or books about Bible topics to read and discuss. There can be some training sessions for those who will lead these studies to help them to know the best things to do. These events not only give members a chance to talk with one another about their needs, problems, and successes, but it can also be a time for members to bring friends to a Bible study.

16. Encourage members who are avid readers to have a daytime book club. They read the same book and come together to discuss it.

17. Parties are a great time for fellowship. Members can decide to have a group of church friends to their home to play card games, domino games, or board games and in the process, the people become better acquainted and feel a stronger bond of fellowship.

18. When a church member has a financial setback, they may need the help of their fellow members. Every congregation should set aside some money in its annual budget to assist members. This is following

HOW THE FELLOWSHIP AT CHURCH *Can be its Best*

the example of the church in Jerusalem. Those whom the church helps will feel a stronger bond with their fellow Christians.

19. Galatians 6:2 says to bear one another's burdens. When a church member loses a loved one, church members should surround that person with love. When a church member loses a job, the church should be there to help. When a church member has an illness or is in the hospital, Christian friends should be there to encourage and to provide assistance as needed. Maybe someone needs to spend the night in the room with the patient because the wife whose husband is recovering has already spent two or three nights there. Christian friends should be present to support a member while a loved one is having surgery. Maybe when the patient comes home, Christian friends can be of special help with meals and other services. Times of burdens are times of opportunity.

20. Older members may live alone who cannot care for all the things at the home and may not be able to afford to pay someone to mow the lawn or clean up the house or even do some things like painting or repairs. When Christian friends do such things, the church becomes aware of what it means to have the fellowship of the saints.

The New Testament often speaks of the oneness, the unity, and the bonds of love that should characterize the church. Of course, the strongest elements in such close links are the faith, the hope, and the love we share. This fellowship, however, can be strengthened by anything that gets us to spend more time together. The elders should be aware of those on the fringe and try to find ways to bring them more to the center of the fellowship.

"There is one body and one Spirit, just as you were called to one hope when you were called; **one Lord, one faith, one baptism**; one God and Father of all, who is over all and through all and in all" (Ephesians 4:4-6, NIV-emphasis added). Our oneness in Christ calls us to fellowship the saints and what a joy it is to live in a community of believers!

ACTION

It is imperative to have an action plan for each item you think should be put into practice. Although the Introduction mentions several ways to do this, it is important for you to determine what steps should be taken to implement the activities you have found while reading this book. The chart below enables you to do that. As you read the book, put a checkmark by those things you hope will be done in your congregation. Then turn to this page, and complete the three columns by listing the page on which the idea is mentioned, then in the middle column, write a brief description of the item, and in the left column, note to whom you should refer the idea of starting this new practice. In that column you may write "me" if you need to be the first one to make the move, or you may write "elders" or the name of the head of the missions committee, or whoever it is to whom you want to refer the item with the hope that it will get started. Good ideas are only good if they get implemented.

PAGE NUMBER	DESCRIPTION	REFER TO

PAGE NUMBER	DESCRIPTION	REFER TO

PAGE NUMBER	DESCRIPTION	REFER TO

www.ingramcontent.com/pod-product-compliance
Lightning Source LLC
Chambersburg PA
CBHW060537100426
42743CB00009B/1549